# Webcentric Local Business Marketing

## How to Market Your Local Business
## on the Web and Beyond

### David M. Sandy, JD.

Critwit Publishing

Memphis

**Webcentric Local Business Marketing**

How to market your local business on the web and beyond

Copyright ©2012 by David Sandy

Because of the dynamic nature of the Internet, any Web addresses or links contained in this book may have changed since publication and may no longer be valid.

ISBN-13: 978-1475093087
ISBN-10:147509308X

Printed in the United States of America

Critwit Publications
731 Litty Ct. #204
Memphis, TN 38103
901-231-1380

# NOTICE

The internet is a rough and tumble place. Search engines can choose to start penalizing any conduct at any time. My information is the best I currently have but I can't eliminate risk and assume no responsibility for being incorrect. Only you can decide if it's a good idea to make a potentially profitable but risky investment.

# Acknowledgments

Thanks to mother for a good editing job, and Dan for encouraging me to finish the thing. Special thanks to some guy from Fiverr for the table of contents and index which would have taken me hours.

# Table of Contents

6

# The Beginning

I remember one day, shortly after I was starting my law practice, I was sitting at my desk surfing the internet and thinking of ideas to market my practice. The phone rang. On the line was a very intriguing salesman from some company in Chicago with a very convincing marketing pitch. For the sum of two thousand or so up front and several hundred a month they'd rank me on the front page for the term "Memphis probate attorney". He showed me how Google search showed several thousand searches a month for the term and a Chicago client on the front page for "Chicago DUI."

I thanked him and decided to investigate more before taking the plunge. I ended up on Elance, found a Romanian outsourcer and got my site to #1 for Memphis lawyer and several other terms within the year for a couple hundred dollars. That was five years ago and that call set me on learning about internet marketing and how to make sites be found in search engines (popularly called "search engine optimization" or "SEO" for short). I now recognize why that phone call was such bad value and one of the most common misleading tactics used in that call.

Small businesses are faced with the most unforgiving and brutal economic environment in recent times. We can't afford to waste money on clueless internet marketers who don't understand what we need to accomplish, who don't care if we make money on their services, and who's lack of knowledge and experience in most cases makes them virtual scam artists.

I'm writing this book as a short, to-the-point guide to empower local business owners and managers to select creditable internet marketers and to verify whether the consultants are actually doing the work. It can also be used as a guide to promoting and managing your own local internet and marketing presence. It's written with a focus on geographically localized businesses such as lawyers, dentists, electricians, restaurants, etc. so it may not be entirely on-point for promoting an ecommerce site for example. It would be useful for someone marketing a national chain with locations, such as Ruth Chris or Hilton.

Local and National search marketing share many of the same tools but are quite different. The number of search terms tends to be much lower. The volume is lower. The competition is lower. Certain forms of testing are not useable due to the lower volume making effective testing difficult. Blogs and social media tend to be much less productive locally.

I've tried to avoid being an internet manual and stick to strategy and tactics. How to sign up for a service or click the right button is usually covered in many effective internet tutorials or much more effectively and succinctly covered in a video format. I've seen a lot of internet guides that really don't seem useful on a strategic or planning level because they turn into a "click here" and "find the menu here" type guide with more pictures than text. Check my website http://www.critwit.com for resources and videos.

## Innovative Marketing Confusion

It's easy to be confused by the wide variety of marketing products available now such as general directory portals (YellowPages.com, yellowbook.com, magicyellow.com, yelp.com, etc.), industry specific portals (avvo.com, zillow.com), social media portals (Facebook.com, Twitter.com, Google+), QR codes, SMS or text message marketing, websites, map/Places optimization, search engine optimization, video marketing, Pay Per Click, mobile websites, advertising on popular websites, Groupon and daily deals, direct response mail, graphic designers, ads in prints media, radio, TV, networking. I'm sure I've omitted some and you need to be aware of how any product will interact with the other products.

At the end of the day this all comes down to the old standby criteria - who's the audience and what's the message.

## Don't Copy Established Businesses

In many cases, established businesses don't approach advertising with the kind of hardnosed Return on Investment approach of the cash strapped expanding startup. I also frequently noticed that other lawyers would praise a certain form of marketing but an examination of the docket would reveal that they weren't actually pulling in the business. I'm not sure this was lying, but I think there's a natural tendency to praise any costly decision to avoid the emotional pain of making a bad decision.

In any case, the good news with modern marketing methods is that they are extremely trackable and targetable. You can view the source of website visits, have specific phone numbers attached to ads, and even track the pages viewed by each visit.

# National vs. Local

One of the signs of a rookie marketing guru is applying national level concepts to local marketing. There's a lot of carryover. There are also some significant differences you'll need to keep in mind mostly related to a vastly lower target market.

- Split testing and most testing in general will be much more difficult due to the smaller numbers involved, making it much harder to obtain valid sample sizes.
- Non-solicited linkbuilding, while overrated even for non-local SEO, has virtually no place in a local SEO strategy.
- It's not a major flaw not to have a social media strategy in all cases; certain niches can effectively ignore social media.
- Social media strategies are more difficult.
- Search engine optimization is far easier with a local scope.
- You will need to target all valid keywords.
- Conversions tend to be higher.
- Large transactions or customer lifetime value.
- You aren't blogging to gain a following but to increase content depth and conversions.

# Brand Market and Direct Response Marketing

There are two main approaches to marketing. The more familiar approach is to build a brand or presence in the hope that when a consumer has a need for a product they will remember you. This is the cute Coke commercial or the Geico Lizard concept. It's the old school marketing you'd hire the guys from *Mad Men* to do for you. This does work in local marketing as well but works best when you've already got a profitable base to start from since it can take years to pay off. In Memphis, there's a law firm which has a fair percentage of the population able to hum their number out to a well known jingle.

Direct response marketing seeks to gain a positive return on investment from any particular ad. This relies on tracking numbers or offers to quantify if a method works. Direct response got its start from direct mail pioneers who compared various formulas for mailing and worked to develop good techniques. Dan Kennedy is perhaps the most well known of these and has many excellent books devoted to the subject.

Local internet centric marketing will be heavily influenced by direct response methodologies though there's going to be some difficultly to qualify brand marketing value.

## The new marketing funnel

It used to be that you'd run an ad, answer the phone and that'd be about be it. The internet has made the process marginally more complex but it is still quite easy.

Now it's

Traffic – Content – Follow-up

Traffic is eyeballs looking at your message. It used to be that traffic was tied to specific advertising expenditures but that's no longer a safe way to think. For example, websites by themselves might be incredible but without a traffic generating strategy they can get virtually no traffic.

Each of these can be broken down into several subject areas. For example, social media sites can generate traffic, contain content, follow-up and maintain relationships. In addition, the internet has given us a website which has the potential to be a potent force multiplier for almost any other ad spend. Whether it's direct mail, social media, radio or YellowPages, a website can increase the effectiveness of almost any advertising both by providing a convenient site for further interaction and by serving as an easily findable depository of contact information.

# Geographic

Certain areas of the country will favor certain media. For example in Memphis, the vast majority of extremely successful lawyers credit television advertising for their initial success. In Nashville, it's YellowPages and print media that rule the day. Memphis also has very low social media usage compared to the rest of the nation. Serious social media success stories tend to happen in techy areas such as the West Coast.

Local based marketing is local, so you'll need to quantify where you are at and factor that into your plans. You'll also need to be prepared to pivot and incur some costs in testing various strategies.

# Research

Researching your competitors is a great idea, but can be misleading. It may seem a great idea to ask your more established peers what works for them, but this is risky. As a lawyer I encountered some incidents of outright lying about what was effective, which I verified by checking the number of cases filed in the online docket. In addition, established business people who are committed to marketing may be spending a certain amount every year without tracking Return on Investment. I've encountered certain lawyers who admitted to this.

Due to issues with scalability, successful businesses might even consciously spend money on less than optimal avenues. For example, a criminal law firm that docket mails all the eligible misdemeanors might buy some very expensive billboards that just breakeven or even lose a little money. This could even make sense for them as their existing volume means that they can service additional business very cheaply and the brand awareness over time makes their docket running results more effective.

# Basic Concepts

Lead – A lead is a potentially interested person who provides some kind of contact information through which you might potentially make a sale.

Conversion Rate - Conversion rate is the rate an interaction graduates to the next metric on the sales funnel. For example, every 10 visits to a website generating a call or lead would be a 10% click to lead conversion rate. Conversion rate should always be stated with what's being converted, for example clicks to leads or leads to sales.

Return on Investment (ROI) - Return on investment for advertising is the amount of net income after variable costs provided by a given advertising investment. Investment not only includes money but also a business owner's time and attention. For example, a yellow page ad may only require a few hours of time a year, but blogging could take several hours a week.

Scalability - Scalability in advertising is advertising where you can increase your spend and theoretically receive a historical return on investment. For example a direct mail campaign where you mailed 1% of the target demographic could be scaled 100x. A non-scalable campaign would be a sign on your physical location or marketing to prior customers. Some advertising might have increasing returns at higher levels and then decreasing.

Scalability is an important consideration in most advertising that requires extensive testing like direct mail.

Lifetime Customer Value – This is probably one of the most important concepts. Hopefully, you should get more than one customer for each one you service based on your advertising through referrals or repeat visits. This can explain why advertising can get bid up so much since a knowledgeable competitor won't just base the expected value on a single sale but on the expected value of all follow-on sales as well.

Cost – This refers to the resources expended for an advertising medium. This should include the time involved by the advertiser in setting up or running the advertising.

Link – A link is an element on a webpage that will lead to a different webpage.

Anchor Text – Anchor text is the words compromising of

a link when not a naked link that is just HTML or possibly a image. Anchor text is a critically important factor in Google rankings.

# Website Setup and Design Issues

## Website design

I have nothing but respect for the best website designers, but as a whole this class probably contains the biggest danger for negative ROI clothed in beautiful aesthetics, with business owners frequently spending 5k on stunningly designed sites lacking a prominent phone number and front page contact form. One of the more effective site designs I ever had was plain text on an off white background I threw together as a placeholder on a discontinued Microsoft web design product called FrontPage.

Quality website design shouldn't be expensive. In the early days of the internet a great site required hours of hand coding. Modern advancements in content management systems and customizable templates have made a quality individualized website design achievable for around five hundred dollars for North American designers, and I've gotten high quality work outsourced for under a hundred.

Structurally, a website is like a brochure. An ability to design and print a nice good looking glossy brochure does not necessarily imply a good ability to distribute the brochure or write the content.

## Website content

Local business content is a different animal than more broadly targeted sites. The major reason is that local business sites are aimed at people with a need who will react quickly. You're not aiming to develop a readership or become a resource. More broadly targeted sites try to do this both for ROI reasons and as an attempt to garner links for SEO purposes.

A good local website covers the essential basics of a description of your services, hours of operation, payments, and a biography of the owner and key employees. You should also have a page specifically titled "privacy policy" since Google might scan for this. Some informative articles are helpful but try not to get carried away. You might want to put these in the form of a blog. A short blog of ten or so entries can be a good site component to increase trust and engage readers.

Local websites should always feature a prominent phone number in the header as well as an easy to find contact button leading to a contact form. It's a good idea to put a contact form on the front page as well. I've found that directly below the content on the front page is particularly effective, if slightly unaesthetic. I've had very poor results with contact forms in the sidebar.

A video embedded within the content can be a good conversion increasing tool, as if viewed there's a lot of evidence that video will lead to contacts over half of the time.

Your website should not include either autoplay music or Flash. Restaurants for some reason are notorious for Flash websites that are annoying and difficult to use, frequently missing a visible hours of operation and menu.

## Blogging

A blog is a chronological list of articles presented on a website. It's a frequently touted tactic and one that's quite frankly overplayed for local marketing. Traditional blogging is basically starting your own periodical. You will need to post every week at a minimum in order to maintain a readership. Blogs lend themselves to SEO as there's a tradition of interlinking between blogs.

This is quite frankly an excessive mistargeted time commitment for local internet marketing and SEO where you're aiming for direct conversions from consumers with an immediate need. I do recommend having a brief blog on sites with helpful articles but you don't need to write regularly and about ten articles will achieve the desired effect of conveying expertise. You can also sign up for a Google Plus account and link your posts and possibly have a small portrait show up by your sites in the search results and increase your click through rates.

You can also use most blog platforms as an interface with social media. There's a WordPress plugin for posting updates to most social media platforms including Facebook and Twitter.

There's an exception to my rule about blogging for locals and that's the local celebrity plan discussed later.

# Website setup options

## URLs

A URL or web address is an alphanumerical name that you own that will resolve to your website. If you didn't have a URL for your website you would use a long string of difficult to remember numbers. Picking a good one is extremely important. If you ever change it you're going to lose a good chunk of your acquired SEO benefits. Some websites allow you to operate a website as a subdomain of their website *i.e.* "www.yoursite.hostingsite.com" If you are going to take the time and effort to develop any internet property you need to get your own domain. It will be extremely hard to switch service providers later on and subdomains may not rank as well as owned domains.

You register a domain at a domain registrar. Domain registrations vary in price but for most extensions you should pay fewer than twenty dollars (if not, shop around). GoDaddy is the most popular registrar and is decent but has expensive privacy protection. If you don't opt for privacy protection the domain owner's info and email will be available and email spammers will send quite a few offers for web related services. In addition, there's a scam where domain registrars will mail renewal bills for domains at inflated rates.

Keywords in a URL will help a site rank for those keywords, especially in Bing. In addition, keywords in the domain might help avoid a penalty for excessive link building since it's very natural to build links using a URL's name as anchor text.

A big thing I see is picking a domain that could only be used by you such as "www.joebobslawfirm.com" etc. This will radically limit your potential to sell the website and by extension your business later on. If you've got a top ranked website generating 30K after twenty years in business, then that's a potential 100K asset sale you might miss out on in selling your business. There is some evidence that personalized URLs can help CTRs but I think that the title tags of websites are a better place for that.

You aren't limited to owning one name. URLs can be forwarded to other main URLs. You might want to have specific alternate URLs to place in ads and the like. This can be a good use for joebobslawfirm.com-type URL's. The only consideration is you might be missing out on some branding effects. If you can't score a great generic .com then placing personalized URL's in advertising can be a good strategy.

# TLDs, .Com and Beyond

A TLD or top level domain is the extension at the end of a domain name. The most famous TLD is .com. There are numerous TLD's available now including .net, .org, .info, and .biz. .com is by far the most valuable and widely used. Most searchers who don't remember that you use a different extension will enter the .com. This means that you can lose a percentage of your business to the .com.

One of the most common pieces of advice in national web marketing is to buy all the extensions of the .com you're planning to develop. This prevents imitators and protects your brand from having a porn site or identity theft scheme on a website with a similar web address as your company. For local SEO of keyword domains, if you're lucky enough to have the .com, you actually want the other extensions developed.

Imagine you owned atlantahomerenovations.com. Joe Renovator couldn't buy yours but decides to buy atlantahomerenovations.pro. He then proceeds to spend a hundred thousand dollars on advertisements with the domain. You'd be real happy with this because probably about five percent of the people who went to enter Joe's

URL would forget it wasn't a .com and find you instead. This scenario wouldn't be applicable if you didn't have a keyword domain and were going for a branded domain names.

There are still a surprising number of decent locally oriented .com's if you take some time. Some tricks to finding an acceptable .com are to include the state postal code *i.e.* memphisTNdivorcelawyer. Put "now" or "hq" at the end of the word e.g. memphisdivorcenow.com. Try not to put a modifier in front of the keywords such as mymemphislawyer.com since this seems to slightly affect search engine results.

## Hosting

A host is a computer server accessible from the internet that makes a webpage available. Selecting a quality host is very important. Good customer service is important since you might have tech problems and viruses come up. Hosting should cost no more than about $16 a month for a small business. You need to make sure your hosting uses a backend called CPANEL since this is the standard backend. Using a CPANEL host will cut down on technical support costs and make it easier to transfer between hosts. Also, make sure your host has a good backup policy, preferably daily with at least a couple months availability of backups.

It's almost a standard newbie thing to go with GoDaddy hosting. They may just be a particular target because of their size but they seemed to me to have an issue with virus infections. When I moved my hosting off of them, I found that my sites speed increased by about 5x.

A more advanced hosting option is a virtual server. This is where the hosting company will effectively partition off your usage. This leads to a potential speed increase, but even more importantly, a greater level of security. The additional cost can be about $40 a month so it's not a priority item for most local businesses, but it is something that should be kept in mind. In addition, there can be some cost to administer the virtual server or increased tech support.

## Keeping the Website Together

Some years ago, most sites were constructed in HTML files usually designed by a web designer and directly uploaded to a webhost. HTML is the markup language that web browsers would read to know what to display. I would not recommend that a small business go with a HTML site anymore. Making any changes at all is a major hassle which frequently requires going back to the website designer (who often disappears).

The trend in modern sites is to go with a system that splits up the content and design element by standardizing the content feeds. A common name for this is a Content Management Systems or CMS. If you change the design the content will stay about the same. There are many systems to accomplish this now. I'm just going to suggest two of them.

## WordPress

WordPress started off as a blogging platform but added the ability to designate a static page as the homepage. This made it useable as a CMS. WordPress is open source and a variety of customizable themes are available that can be easily adjusted for a custom look. It also basically forces you to use a good internal linking structure for SEO purposes. A number of plugins have also been developed to add functionality, from calendars, to statistics, to automatically creating a mobile version of your website to Twitter feed inserts.

There is also a large online community so if you Google a potential issue there's a good chance you're going to find someone who's had the same issue and a resolution too.

The biggest downside to WordPress is that it's incredibly vulnerable to hacking. Partly because, like Windows, it's the most popular platform it gets the most number of hackers because it's the most bang per evil buck. It also has a large number of popular plugins that aren't vetted consistently, and it's database driven. There are also apparently ways to hack hosting accounts and get all the sites on a shared host. At a very minimum you'll need to keep the most current update on your install (and there are a lot of updates!). This makes WordPress ill-suited for websites that won't be changed weekly or more often.

If you get a WordPress site make sure all references to the word "WordPress" are removed from the site. Hackers use scanning software to scan for footprints in order to locate blogs to try to hack, and WordPress powered sites are a popular footprint.

## Weebly

Weebly is a drag and drop website application that has a variety of customizable themes and functions somewhat like WordPress. A major exception is that it compiles the results into an HTML file so it's much more secure than WordPress and easier to maintain. The site will usually load quite snappy, though since I moved off GoDaddy it's not a significant improvement. It's a site with a lot of small business use so it's actually much easier to set up tracking and contact forms than WordPress. You have to sign up for the Weebly Pro if you don't want a little Weebly button in the bottom middle of the site.

You can download the file from Weebly and upload it onto your own hosting account if you wish. Weebly also acts as a very creditable web host and includes hosting for up to ten sites in the PRO version.

There's a service called squarespace.com that seems better than Weebly, but they charge by site which, since I always have a bunch of projects going on, isn't feasible for me personally.

## Mobile Websites

A good percentage of searches will be conducted on cell phones. Most websites don't perform well on the small screen space. Now web designers have a new market of offering streamlined sites that are mobile optimized.

Weebly and some WordPress themes will be mobile optimized by default. Check your website on a smartphone before you commit to spending money on a mobile optimized site. If it's not a mobile optimized site, there's a plugin for WordPress called WP Mobile Pro that will configure a mobile optimized version. A hand designed mobile optimized version should be reasonable if you don't want to use the plugin or really want to go fancy with the smartphone users.

## Finding Out What's Going On
*Tracking*

## Google Analytics and Webmaster Tools

Google offers two free services for monitoring a websites' performance. 'Google Analytics' tracks click data and 'webmaster tools' will show website-related links, sitemaps, and query data. When you register for a Gmail account you'll be able to add more products including these two. You will get a code when you register that will need to be inserted in the footer of your site. WordPress has specific plugins to help you do this and most drag and drop editors will have specific instructions and a page where you can do this too.

Most internet marketers avoid Google's tools due to a fear that Google might cross-reference more aggressive tactics used by a site with others in the same account. These fears don't apply as much to a local business who won't have a large number of sites. You should always have any outside help setup a separate account for you and give you the password.

Google webmaster tools can display the number of times your website appears for certain search terms, the number of links to your site, and most importantly will potentially warn you about site infections. You can also use it to upload a site map to help Google find all your site pages.

Google analytics tracks data. You can view hits over a large span of time by daily, monthly, and yearly intervals. You can change this view to 'view by traffic type' such as keyword, referring site, and search. I find the keyword data to be less reliable than StatCounter, and I believe Google may be displaying phrase matches. The traffic graphing is slightly better and Google keeps the data going back indefinitely at this point. It's also slightly more difficult to track visitor paths in Google Analytics than StatCounter.

There is some argument that Google may at times

present incorrect data on some of its services, particularly the incoming link data on Webmaster Tools.

## StatCounter.com

StatCounter is a website visit tracker that is similar to Google Analytics. It's free for up to a log of 500 visits which is a lot for local search. I prefer its visitor log, keyword tracking and summary over Google analytics, but the graphing is a little off and doesn't work as well with subsets. The keyword data is very useful though as you can find terms that get quite a few visits, and if you aren't ranked at #1 then focus on those terms.

## Open Site Explorer

opensiteexplorer.org is a tool presented by SEOMOZ.org, a very well respected SEO consulting firm (I personally don't agree with them on everything but they always have an interesting read). I consider it the gold standard for measuring the quantity and quality of incoming links. It will also tell you the number of sites linking in, which is of crucial importance as a site-wide link that is on every page of a site might show 1000's of links on other tools. You'll need to register to do more than 1 search per day. You also won't be able to view all of the links without a very expensive subscription. You really don't need to look at the links though; it's the aggregate data that matters. Basically, SEOMOZ has their own robot programs crawling the internet and finding links. They compile this once per month. I find their data to be the most credible and reliable measure of your link building success. They display the links by their link popularity ranking for the linking site and page.

It's also a great tool for checking out the competition and keyword research.

## Traffic Travis

Traffic Travis is a free tool with a pro version that's the best way to keep track of keywords your rankings are targeting. You basically just enter your website and a list of keywords for it to check. If you had multiple projects or a very long list it might time out as Google could temporarily block your IP address for automated queries. They also have a competition research tool that will display a top 10 or top 20 list for a chosen phrase and pertinent statistics for the ranking sites. I would warn Traffic Travis users that the link data may not be reliable as it comes from Yahoo site explorer and will count site-wide links as individual links.

# Search Engine Marketing

Search engine marketing is a blanket term for marketing a business using search engines as the primary traffic source. I'd categorize the major elements as search engine optimization (SEO) and Pay Per Click (PPC). I'm not big on this term as it primarily seems a limited use guru lingo term with too much overlap with other good terms, yet too narrow to be useful in a wider sense. I really prefer website marketing for an umbrella term encompassing SEO, PPC, referring internet media, and using traditional media to drive traffic to the site.

## Understanding Local Search Results

A local search can be defined as one with Geographic Intent. It's estimated that up to 60% of searches might fall under this. Originally, Google didn't provide strong tools catering to the local market and treated geographic modifiers as essentially another keyword.

This changed with the introduction of Google Places around 2008. Google's search results had consisted of two segments. A paid section called Adwords at the top in some cases and on the side.

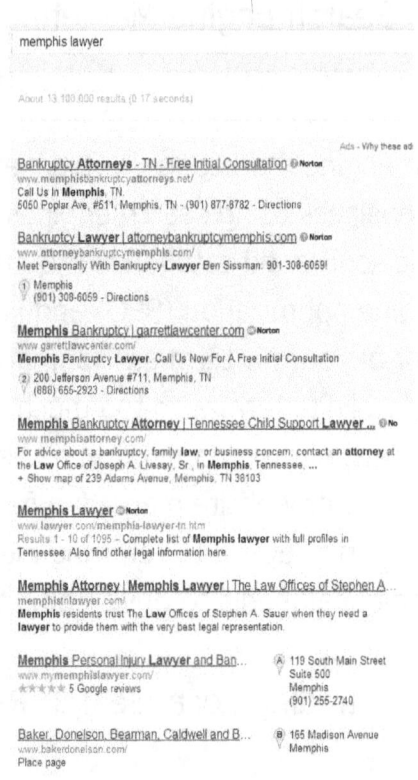

(Typical local search result with Adwords results, web results, and Places results below.)

Now Google inserts local results from its database of local businesses called Google Places or Maps when it detects a probable local search. These are generally displayed with their address and with a little flag on the map. These results can draw up to 60% or so of organic search volume. The rankings of these Places results appears to be largely independent of traditional links or

SEO.

Google has been monkeying with this for several years. The latest iteration appears to effectively blend the ranking when the SEO and the associated Places listing will give close results. If the SEO for a website outranks a Places listing it now seems possible for the organic site to outrank the Places results.

Importantly, you might in some cases get a double listing with both a website and good Google Places page. Pure blending seems to occur most often for highly SEO'd results where many rankings would appear in top positions for both their SEO and Places rank.

In addition, Google has moved recognition of when a search is location based beyond the keywords involved. Google will pick up on the IP address of the computer performing the search and display local SEO and Places results intermixed with regular results when it thinks people are looking for a local service. This means that when you search for "bankruptcy lawyer" and you are located in Atlanta you will see local websites that you wouldn't see with a New York search.

# SEO

## White hat, black hat, and no hat

There's a big trend about warning people of the dangers of black hat SEO. I find most of these warnings to be disingenuous. Technically anything that violates the Google webmasters term of service could be considered black hat. I rarely find anyone espousing white hat tactics with competitive search results who actually uses pure white hat techniques. If you view the Google TOS you can see why.

> "These quality guidelines cover the most common forms of deceptive or manipulative behavior, but Google may respond negatively to other misleading practices not listed here (e.g. tricking users by registering misspellings of well-known websites). It's not safe to assume that just because a specific deceptive technique isn't included on this page, Google approves of it. Webmasters who spend their energies upholding the spirit of the basic principles will provide a much better user experience and subsequently enjoy better ranking than those who spend their time looking for loopholes they can exploit."

There is very little you can do to effectively promote a website that wouldn't fall astray of this somehow. There's even a catchall provision like the inappropriate behavior infraction at my state sponsored boarding high school back in the day. Any intentional link building, even relevant link exchanges could technically be black hat.

The funny thing is that the biggest scam I encounter in SEO is what I refer to as the no hat SEO scheme. This occurs when SEO's charge high monthly fees and do virtually nothing except adjust tags which takes maybe thirty minutes of setup and five minutes to send a monthly report. They usually studiously warn their clients about the dangers of black hat SEO's and stay pure and virtuous by engaging in no link building whatsoever. As it happens, link building is by far the most time and money intensive step of the SEO process. They usually have no chance of achieving positive results in a niche with any competition.

Actual documented cases of Google link building penalties were extremely rare and aren't common in local. The most well-known case involved J. C. Penney. In early 2011 some tech bloggers noticed that J. C. Penney had the number one position for a wide swatch of consumer goods. This was a result of a large number of links established just before the holiday shopping season.

They convinced a reporter at the *New York Times* to take a look at the situation. This resulted in a story implicating the company. Google were forced to take action or would appear to be actively condoning the behavior, so they implemented some algorithmic changes and penalized J.C. Penney what appeared to be -50 on all their search terms. J.C. Penney denied all culpability of linking and blamed its SEO consultant for unauthorized activity and removed the offending links. (A great strategy for all big companies caught doing aggressive SEO). About six weeks later the penalties were lifted.

The white hat and no hat SEO experts crowed about this. To me this says that in order to get penalized you need to engage in a massive clumsily deployed scheme with an obvious footprint (the link all had hidden source code saying they were bought) and have a *New York Times* story written about it. There are some reports I've heard that I consider somewhat credible, saying that it's possible to trigger a filter in competitive niches via link building that causes a manual review. The review might manually penalize a site if the reviewers found it was a thin, low content site promoting affiliate offers.

In any case, this is not the kind of thing you need to get concerned about when doing local SEO which is relatively low competition for everything, but possibly concern yourself if you are in law and real estate in very large cities. Being the feature of a New York Times article is a risk that most small local businesses would be okay running.

In terms of actual legalities, Google isn't a government entity or at this point has regulatory control over the internet. Certain tactics such as automated blog spam may constitute an actionable business interference tort of some type depending on the state.

## Search engines

A search engine is a website that categorizes other websites and delivers a list of websites in response to a query.

At this time there are two significant search engines, Bing/Yahoo and Google. Yahoo is owned by Bing and runs their results. Standard practice is to optimize for Google and Bing/Yahoo will tend to follow. Google receives about 2/3rd's of the traffic officially and Bing/Yahoo about 1/3rd. I've never had a website go above about 20% for Bing/Yahoo so I'm actually a little skeptical of that figure. The traffic from Bing might be a bit higher with commercial intent traffic.

There are minor search engines that receive a small amount of traffic but at this time they aren't worth mentioning.

## How Google Ranks Sites

Google is of course a black box. No one outside of Google knows exactly what they're doing. However, after you've ranked a few sites over a period of years you begin to get a good feeling for it.

I'm guessing the following is a pretty good description of how the results for a particular term would look.

Search Term Score = (Onpage Score ^ Generic Link Power)+ Anchor Text Link Score

This is, of course, a rough approximation but what it vaguely means is that you must link build, but on page factors aren't going to get you there if there's competition.

This leads to the general rule that for virtually all local terms you can achieve good results for SEO purposes with link building and ignore the on page factors. A term doesn't even have to appear on the site to rank for it in Google. This doesn't seem to be true for Bing and makes Bing rankings a much more expensive and difficult proposition than ranking for Google. Since Bing is a much smaller market than Google anyway, standard practice is to rank for Google, which will usually accomplish most of what could be done for Bing anyway. Bing also appears to treat on page and especially URL as much more important factors. This has the effect of fracturing the broadness you can target with the site and dramatically lowers the return on investment.

On page SEO is extremely inexpensive, however, and basically just consists of marking up the correct text with the right HTML.

## Suspected On Page Optimization Factors

Title - The title attribute is the most important factor on a web page. Google will give it a ranking power and will usually display it in the search results. This leads to more rookie local SEO's keyword stuffing the title tag. It's much more important to have it look natural. I prefer a good keyword followed by a local phone number. Local phone numbers have been shown to increase click through rates in Adwords and I believe they work in regular SEO. Google has been experimenting with finding text on the page to match a search term, so the title tag is more difficult to work with than in the past.

Metadata - The metadata tag can be used to generally describe what a site is ranking for.

Site Size – Google does seem to be adverse to ranking pages on small sites. I find that my best rankings on local terms come with sites above ten pages of content.

Site Age – The age a domain has been indexed in Google.

Page Age – The length of time a page has been indexed in Google seems important.

H1, H2, H3, quotes, italics, underlining – These are HTML attributes you can use to emphasize text or mark it as a heading. There may be some slight positive effect for the text with these attributes so it's worth keeping in mind if you can work it in without sacrificing user experience.

Keyword Density – This used to be a big one but at this point I'd say it's important to use a phrase 1-2 times, as anything more is probably unnecessary.

Freshness – The frequency of updates can be very influential, and this is one of the reasons why blogs can do well.

Internal Linking – Internal links pass value and relevancy. You should absolutely try to use anchor text links to interior pages for terms you are trying to rank for.

## Keyword Research

Keyword research is the base level of SEO. It's importance tends to be overblown for Local SEO because most SEO professionals come from an internet marketing background where it's absolutely critical (or if you're not lucky, your consultant comes from a sales background and hasn't SEO'd a competitive term in their life). In internet marketing you look for terms with a good reward/work ratio and build sites around those terms. For local internet marketing the subject of a site is already set and the customer value and low competition means you're going to want to optimize for virtually all terms with any significant volume.

The basic keyword research tool is the Google search tool, which is accessed by signing up for an Adwords account. Numerous other keyword tools exist but most of them access this data and repackage it in an easier to use format. They all cost money and to my mind shouldn't be considered for someone who's not in the business of optimizing sites. I've never used any of them.

Basically, once you've accessed the tool you enter a combination of likely terms and Google will return prospective search volume. For local search this will generally be easy. Locality + terms. Try every combination, order will matter. Remember to search for all the services you do, but generally the big ones will be obvious.

Also, search "service in city", "service in city + state postal code (*e.g.* tn)". Once you've entered the terms and asked for the result Google will spit out a table like this. Go to the left hand side and change the results from Broad Search to Exact Search. In major metro areas it can be profitable to search for major suburbs as well.

This is one of the more important facts that no

one seems to tell you in SEO. Google displays data for search terms using different criteria for calculations. Broad match refers to every search term that Google, by some mysterious hand-waving, concludes might have something to do with the search term. Phrase match refers to a search that includes the term. Exact search is exactly what it sounds like and the best data.

Broad match can be 100x times higher than Exact match in some cases. It's a favorite SEO scam tactic of shady firms to show broad match results and then talk about how there are 5000 people searching for "Chicago plumbing" on Google or some such when the actual number might be 100.

Then you can export this table to Excel for future reference. It might be necessary to run several tables and combine them.

Plain text = broad match
"text in quotes" = phrase match
[text in brackets] = exact match

Unfortunately, for local search results, Google can be fishy. Actual results for impressions from webmaster tools can vary some. It's still the best/only real tool around with somewhat solid numbers, though Yahoo has recently released a product called Yahoo Clues that offers some variety.

Another technique is the Google autocomplete feature. When you start typing in "city + service" it'll offer suggestions that other people have searched. No one is exactly sure how this works but some people report success in using it for keyword research. Every outlying area could also potentially have decent volume.

Overall, keyword research is an important first step. It can be worthwhile to purchase a report from a keyword research specialist. They usually cost about $10 off a forum such as WarriorForum with complex reports costing around $50 where the keyword is compared with multiple surrounding localities.

## Penalties, Penalties, and the Sandbox

Google can give penalties to sites for a variety of transgressions. The most severe is deindexing. It's usually given to sites that employ redirects (especially to off-topic porn or pharmacy). This penalty is reported to wear off after two or so years. If you enter the query 'site:yoursite.com' and nothing comes up, you might be deindexed.

The good thing about most Google penalties

except deindexing is that they historically wear off. Excess link building penalties are widely acknowledged to be the least severe. The more severe penalties tend to relate to dishonest and seemingly bad behavior seen from the early days of the internet. Thin one page sites setup for a specific keyword to exploit URL name rankings called landing pages, links colored to be invisible, and other related wonky techniques have very little benefit and can all cause problems.

Excess link building penalties seem to be in the category of a caution flag. It's widely acknowledged that if Google permanently penalized excess link building it'd open the door to people spamming the competition and general snarkiness. The current setup seems to be that you can temporarily harm sites but over time the links would actually benefit the site.

An organic penalty does not mean your site can't be typed in or advertised on Adwords. It also doesn't appear to affect Places results, though those have their own penalties. Given that you'd probably be getting no traffic if you didn't SEO it's a false economy to freak out about penalties. Google also doesn't have broader internet police powers so even if they deindex your site completely, your email and direct type ins should still work.

The sandbox is a special type of penalty/filter that Google is widely believed to apply to new sites. After a short period (about two months) of decent rankings, a site could disappear to the bottom of the results, and it could take up to a year to reappear. It was said that you could avoid this by linkbuilding very carefully. I didn't believe this for a while, but then again I developed a dedicated local bankruptcy site, built it up very slowly and never entered the Sandbox. It still took a year to start achieving first page rankings however so I'm not sure not if entering the Sandbox was a big deal. In fact, dowsing links harder would have made the site probably more powerful later on.

## How many links?

It's really hard to tell people how many links they can build. A 5000 link automated blast might have 30 links Google actually picks up on. Based on experience I'm going to base it on a dollar amount. I think purchased wholesale you'll be safe with under two hundred dollars a month in non-automated links and automated bookmarking or article submissions. I think around ten dollars a month in automated blog or forum links to buffer sites is about the maximum I'd possibly recommend for a local site. I actually don't recommend automated links at all at this point for any site unless you are very experienced. I'd say that for every year of link building you could safely increase this amount by fifty percent.

I'm not including network fees unless they include links. You should also vary the anchor text and not target a limited number of phrases. Building links to more broad non-local terms is very valid and will increase the number of terms you are targeting, and since Google will give local sites a boost for searches with local IP's, it will help you to rank for the broad term in your area.

## Evaluating a Link

A link can be worth $2000/month or a one off fee of .0001¢. Part of the art of SEO is evaluating linking opportunities which may come and go as web properties decide what they're going to offer and at what price. Here are some factors you should use.

Age Site – Links on older sites are probably worth more.

Age Page - Links on older pages are probably worth more.

Age Link - The older a link the more it is worth. This means links that might stick around for years or decades would be much more valuable.

Original Content - Sites with original content may give more powerful links.

Number of Outgoing links - The number of outgoing links can be important. This number is hard to pin down. I'd say 20 is clearly safe, 50 a bit risky, and more than that a significant devaluation.

Relatedness of Outgoing Links - This probably matters more than number even. A site linking to a number of topically unrelated sites is much more likely to be selling links. Google has recently begun introducing an over-optimization filter that may be targeting links from unrelated content, so this is a very important factor to watch.

Quality of Outgoing Links - Sites linking to higher quality sites give higher quality links. If a site has ten links to the likes of CNN and Wikipedia, that's the company you'd be glad to be seen among. Conversely if a site has a large number of anchor text links to crummy sites (like the kind seen in auto-approve blog comments) my experience is they won't count for much.

Actual Site - An actual functioning site is a more valuable link then a made for links site, all else equal. The more a site looks potentially real and aesthetically, pleasing the higher I'd rate it in this category.

Incoming Off-page Links – This is a measure of the number and quantity of links incoming to a page. You can usually view this using tools like 'opensiteexplorer.org'.

Indexed - Google maintains two indexes. A search index that is searched and a bigger supplemental index that maintains content not deemed worthy of inclusion into the search index. It is widely held but not a verified belief among SEO experts that links in the main index are more valuable. I personally believe that a link source that doesn't achieve links in the main index is probably not overly valuable, though many other factors would correlate with if a link's page is in the main index.

PageRank Site - A site with a homepage PageRank is probably going to be better than a site with no homepage PageRank. In addition, an older site with no PageRank might be penalized.

Freshness of Page with Links - Links on frequently updated pages would be more valuable then links on static pages.

Platform - Due to ease of use and development of auto posting tools most bought links come on WordPress platforms. Therefore, I'd value links on WordPress sites slightly less.

Automation - Links created through automated methods are generally less valuable.

Location of Links - Google has described various patents and methods to give different weight based on location. The best location is within content on a page. Other options include footer, widget, comment, and etc. It's a favorite tactic of wannabe internet SEO gurus to proclaim that various links no longer work based on Google or established SEO expert's commenting that they are lessening the weighting of certain links. At this point virtually all locations including in content can be credibly said to have had their weight lessened at some time. Most recently the ease of ranking quickly with high quality links seems to have been reduced.

Content of Page Header Link Is On - I'm not sure if this affects Google, but it's widely held to be a Bing factor.

Anchor text - Anchor text on a link will help with ranking a specific keyword and possibly related keywords.

IP Addresses - An IP address is used to identify a website, so you want maximum diversity in this.

## It's good to be followed

In response to more aggressive link building techniques Google has introduced a no-follow tag that websites may use to indicate to Google that they aren't endorsing the links with that tag. You'll encounter no-follow tags most frequently in blog comment areas and forums, though potentially any link might have it. You'll want it explicitly agreed with potential link sellers that your link is to be do-follow. If you view page source a no-follow link will look like so:

```
<a href="http://www.example.com/" rel="nofollow">Link text</a>
```

There's some argument that having exclusively do-follow links might be indicative of contrived linkbuilding so it won't hurt to get some no-follow links, but you're mainly after do-follow.

## Evaluating a Link Profile

You'll want to employ a good variety of links. SEO's generally believe that Google looks at the quality of links in aggregate. Google probably looks at these factors in evaluating a link profile.

Link Velocity - Google seems to and logically responds to a consistent multi-month or year linking program. I don't think a day to day consistency is necessarily the thing but it's good to have links going out at least weekly. Include anchor texts such as phone number and typical generics such as "click here" for about twenty percent of links.

Anchor Text Variety – It's good and more natural to have a wide variety of potential anchor text. I'd aim for at least 20 potentials.

Variety of Incoming Link Power or PR – Google seems to reward sites that have a mix of low, medium, and high quality links.

Different Types of Links - Google probably rewards a variety of different types of links as more natural.

## Spinning

Spinning is a uniqueness enhancement technique that utilizes infrequently used punctuation symbols to mark up a document to produce a large number of original variants. The most commonly used symbols are | and { and }.

Take a sentence like.

A dog chased the cat.

You can mark off different possibilities in {} separated by |.

A {dog|chimp} {chased|ate|licked} the {cat|dolphin|truffle}.

A computer program would then create however many unique versions of this by selecting an option inside each bracket at random. You can nest brackets to put different variants on sentence and paragraph level. The above example could produce unique original thoughts such as:

A dog ate the cat.
A chimp licked the dolphin. Etc.

Numerous link building techniques require content

for execution. Google tends to treat unique content more kindly and spinning offers a way to dramatically reduce the cost of originality. There is some belief that Google may not view spinning as creating quality unique content and can discount instances where it happens, possibly issuing a filter/penalty.

This means that spinning has quality concerns. If you're going to use spinning I'd suggest at a minimum three variations of each sentence, as well as word level spinning. An interesting technique is to write three articles of a set number of paragraphs on the same topic and interchange them.

## PageRank

PageRank is a mathematical algorithm named after Larry Page used to identify the relative importance of a web page based on the number of links leading to it. It is used in the Google algorithm in some nebulous manner to help in ranking web pages.

If you've spent a large amount of time analyzing search results you'll realize that PageRank isn't critical for a well-ranking website for a particular term. If you do effective link building your PageRank will rise eventually. Google will display the PageRank on the Google toolbar and updates it infrequently, no more than once a quarter. Google once went a year without a serious update and caused all sorts of fuss and panic.

Google quite obviously, and they state this, no longer uses the original PageRank algorithm. There's clearly a time element involved for one, I can state from experience that a link building campaign will lower PageRank on an established site for around 3-6 months before it goes back up. This means that you can get relative deals on younger sites.

The major use of PageRank is in evaluating sites and pages for link building purposes. The link selling market in particular will usually price links by PageRank. You should be aware that PageRank of a site's homepage is frequently used by link sellers to misrepresent the value of links they are selling. A disreputable seller may place a link on a page with no rank and then set a price based on a well ranked homepage. This is made more confusing by a frequently held belief among some SEO's that a link from a site with some homepage PageRank, even on a unranked page, is more valuable than a link on a site with an unranked homepage.

To complicate matters even further it's possible to fake PageRank with a variety of techniques. PageRank can also act as a tipoff that the page is being penalized in some way for selling links.

Overall, Pagerank is something to be aware of but it's not particularly important. I use it as a quick reference to decide if I want to look into something in more depth. Before I procure a link that will require a fair amount of resources I'm going to go to a site like www.opensiteexplorer.org and evaluate the incoming links. This is much more accurate and way safer.

## Negative SEO

Starting in 2012, Google has started actually punishing questionable link profiles. While I don't think it is no longer viable to link build, since without it you won't go anywhere, it's now important to be much more careful.

If you are ranking in a competitive space you need to be prepared for negative SEO attacks that might sideline your site for extended periods of time. SEO still has a great return, but the risk has increased. The upside of all this is that it now requires a much lower volume of links to rank.

# Link Building Techniques

## Directories

Site directories have been around for quite a while. Basically these are website that list and categorize other websites. While you could construct ways that this could go wrong with Google, to my mind it's one of the safest means of linkbuilding. There are even videos of Matt Cutts pondering why people didn't use the technique more.

It's spam free in that the site owners are actually set up to be accepting links. In addition, your link is probably going to be in a category of related sites thus increasing your relevancy.

Two directory sites have acquired a special reputation and bear mention. DMOZ.org or the Open Directory Project was started in 1998, attempting to categorize all the relevant quality websites. It is run by a large number of uncompensated editors, and it is noted for giving quality links. Unfortunately, the submission process is extremely random. Certain categories may not have an active editor or the editor might be a competitor who doesn't approve any listings. I'd advise submitting your site once finished and just not worrying about it. Try not to use a keyword rich anchor as it will be seen as spammy.

The Yahoo directory is also noted and I've seen well ranking sites that use it. It's also quite expensive at $299/year for a commercial submission currently. It does let you use a keyword rich anchor. It's possible that if you don't pay the renewal Yahoo won't get around to deleting your entry but there's no guarantee of that.

Various YellowPages and local business guides also count as directories, though usually with no anchor text. These are critical for your Places page and are usually high quality links. I would categorize a submission to these as an essential part of an online strategy and will discuss them more in the Google Places chapter.

Overall, I think directories are a great SEO strategy. There are a large variety of free and paid listings options, but overall they tend not to be powerful enough to achieve results in competitive categories alone. I would definitely recommend them as a part of any strategy and I think SEO without them is deficient, as they dramatically improve the quality of most link profiles to outside observers.

# Blog Comments

Though the ability to comment on blogs has gone down due to people shutting comments off to combat link spammers, blogs have come to be regarded as a primary link source. Most blog platforms offer the ability for a commentator to leave in their comment a link back to their personal website. This dates from the cooperative wiki-like nature of the early internet and was designed with the idea that a community of interacting bloggers would develop.

SEO experts realized that they could get links on these platforms and gradually overran them with automated software. This led to the development of the no-follow attribute that allowed blog owners to specify that left links weren't to be counted by Google.

Unfortunately, at this point I have to say that automated linking using blog comments can still work. I don't personally have any sites using this technique successfully but I've examined the link profiles of sites for some competitive terms and they are definitely using automated blog commenting. These sites are all quite old though, so my informed opinion is that for local SEO you'd be looking at a long time investment. My experiments with the technique showed no quick results and rarely would the links show on webmaster tools.

What did show up with a high frequency were longer manual comments on moderated sites I made myself. This technique also has the advantage of being less spammy, though certain webmasters are on a rampage against any form of contrived linkbuilding.

There are various directories of blog and you can use a Google search of a "topic blog" to find candidates for commenting. A more advanced method of finding blogs to comment on is to use a tool called Scrapebox that can comb the internet for specific text and footprints that might be good candidates for commenting. I think this would be overkill for a small business owner to fool with however and you could get a better return by spending the software license fee on services.

Overall, I think a small amount of blog commenting is okay, but I wouldn't use it as a primary source for links. If you are surfing the internet and find something you feel like, leave a comment on it. I would advise you to fill out the link section of the comment form. If you decide to purchase blog comments, make sure the commentator leaves original comments at least several sentences long.

## Forum Links

Forums are websites setup to facilitate discussions. These will usually be topic specific. Most forums require that users register and create a profile. This profile can usually contain one or two links. If you are leaving links in a profile make sure the profile contains unique content or else I'm fairly sure it's going to get dropped from the index.

Profile links have very little value and most individuals who use them will set up a special backlink indexer website in order to strengthen them. They do have some effect that's difficult to quantify. I bought 10k links one time to point at an experiment site. That was a long time project and it cratered over a hundred positions.

If you are active on a forum you will usually be able to put links in the bottom of all your posts, called a 'signature'. These can be moderately effective but for local SEO I wouldn't bother unless you are already active on a forum.

# Article

Early on in the history of the internet, entrepreneurs sought to develop informational websites at a low cost. Paying writers and editors is expensive so they devised a method of gathering information cheaply called crowd-sourcing. *Pro bono* work is tough to get consistently so these sites offered the ability to plant 1-3 links for each article someone posted on a site. Authors would benefit not only from the link power offered but from the higher authority of these sites which could make the article rank and get traffic on its own. In addition, some of these sites made all the articles available for posting on other sites so your article stood a chance of going viral and attracting more links and traffic than the original listing on its own.

These articles would typically be 300-1000 words. Over the years, this system devolved into these sites containing millions of non-interlinked shallow and repetitive articles being written by third world outsourcers. Then, spinning could be applied to the article and run through software that would post a unique spun version to 1000's of these "informational sites".

These sites would make their money based on a Google product called "adsense" that displayed contextual advertising. The more content they had the greater the chance it would come on a Google search and someone would view it and click on an adsense ad. This meant that they had little or no incentive to police content since the marginal cost of adding an additional page to an automated page is close to zero. The sites came to be known derisively as "content farms" for their raising of vast crops of nearly unintelligible data. This was a problem because some of these sites were quite old and powerful and Google liked to rank the resulting articles quite highly, since Google liked big and old sites. In addition, these directory sites could acquire quite a few links since people would pass around lists of good article directories to get links from.

In the end there was public outcry and eventually Google reacted with something called the Panda/Farmer updates that applied some sort of filter to identify "content farm" sites. This resulted in dramatic traffic and revenue drops to most of these sites. Certain SEO wannabes started trumping without testing or looking at rankings that this was the end of article marketing for link building purposes. My sites and rankings that used article links remained steady so I'd say that this is not true. The rankings of the pages may have changed but their link power remained the same.

Ezinearticles.com is the oldest and probably the

most powerful of these sites. It was known for applying the highest editorial standards. Many SEO's would hand place the original non-spun seed articles in Ezine and use automation for the rest. After Panda, Ezine raised its standards, but it still has not regained former glory.

I'm not as big a fan as I was of article marketing but I still think it should be a mainstay of local SEO due to the cost and relative quality of the links. I don't think it would rank in the top 3 strategies since it used to have the advantage that you could rank the articles you submitted in the better directories as a separate web property. This was a great advanced strategy to have multiple spots in the front page of results.

## Web 2.0

Web 2.0 is a highly related strategy to article marketing. In the more general form Web 2.0 refers to web properties that offer a social or collaborative element. In the SEO world, web 2.0's are sites that offer the possibility of posting your own content on a personalized subdomain. Key examples include Google's Blogger, Tumbler, and Blog.com.

The advantage over article marketing is that you

can post several layers of articles and also add images. This means 2.0's can have a much less contrived look. In addition, 2.0's have not been hit as hard by the Panda update so they can usually be individually ranked much more easily. They do need to be ranked carefully; most 2.0 providers monitor these sites and may deindex them for excessive linkbuilding.

Overall, web 2.0's have a definite place. I would recommend posting at least 3-4 articles on each property you intend to use. Some link sellers selling web 2.0 links will set up properties with 1 article and no sidebar or images, and these don't index as well and have a tendency to get flagged as link spam and deindexed.

If you are looking for more control you can spend the money and purchase dedicated URL's. Some 2.0 services (Blogger and WordPress) will allow you to use your own URL. If your 2.0 gets deindexed you can just move it. The ultimate in control will involve setting up your own hosting for these sites at which point they're referred to as a private blog network.

### Press Release

Press releases are basically a high quality form of article marketing. Unlike article marketing it does need to be something actually news worthy, preferably about your business. If you are giving a speech, it's a great time for a press release. In a pinch you can make a press release about local news such as housing starts if you are in real estate for example. You then distribute the press release through a service such as PRWeb, although some services will not allow anchor text links.

## Private Blog Networks

Private blog networks probably rank as the most powerful and cost effective option for local SEO. Basically, SEO firms and resellers amass a number of site on which they set up WordPress blogs that can accept content via a front end or an autoposter. It's also possible that groups would collaborate and each contribute sites in exchange for access to the system or that blog could sign up to receive content in order to have frequent and updated content.

These systems range from truly private small networks owned by an SEO consultant to open networks that charge a monthly fee for posting access.

These networks have a variety of features and differences to optimize, in their owners minds, their effectiveness and cost. Some buy sites that people are letting expire and have acquired PageRank. They then repurpose it to be used in the blog network in hopes that these sites won't have their incoming links pulled and their outgoing links would be more valuable. At the other end of the spectrum, there are networks that buy 1000's of 1.99$ .info domains (some TLD's have a discount the first year to encourage use) to post to. They then let them expire every year and hopefully roll the blogs over onto new TLD's. This makes me nervous as Google tends to reward age and stability over all else when it comes to links.

The volume advocates argue that as new posts push posts off the PageRanked homepage that all the links will be on PR 0 pages anyway, but I do believe that site PR does matter by itself and passes to most pages to some degree, even if unmeasured.

Other frequently encountered differences include requiring original or spun content, limiting the number of posts so the link power is not spread as thinly and posts stay longer on the more powerful homepages, supporting blog posts with automated link building techniques like social bookmarking or RSS feeds to auto blogs, if ads are put on the pages, disclosure of where the links are, and degree of hosting diversity. Generally, the more of any conservative sounding difference, the more powerful a network will be. The most powerful easy to access network I use with the most impressive results requires original content, no ads, supports each post, and has private hosting. The only rival in terms of effectiveness are smaller truly private networks ran by individuals, which are usually nice but have scalability issues.

On all these blog networks it's fairly standard that your posts will remain indefinitely. This is of course aspirational and cannot be effectively guaranteed. As a practical matter, the near zero memory costs of adding another text based page to a website means that as long as the operator keeps the sites up he'll probably keep your posts up. These networks do cost money to maintain so the possibility remains of a deletion. This means a best practice is to use a variety of these networks for link building in addition to signing up for quality networks that sound like they'll be able to offer value for awhile and sustain themselves.

The downside to most of the networks is that they have such a wide variety of linked sites that it would be fairly easy to construct a relevancy filter to identify them. I've personally thought of developing networks for specific niches and only allowing posts that were related. That way you could develop websites that would be indistinguishable from real functioning sites.

Using these sites is fairly easy: you pay the money to get access and then write an article, insert the link and post it. The link is placed in the content which is the most valuable place to have a link. It's suggested that the link go in the upper third of an article. This is because most article directories don't allow links in the main article body but require them in the footer. This may have led Google to treat links in the bottom part of a text as less valuable. If you connect with someone with a private network they'll generally have a dedicated writer and handle it all for you.

There's another variant of these networks called 'homepage back link networks'. These networks buy PR'd sites and instead of putting a blog with transient posts on the homepage they put an article there and cram between 5-100+ links into it. They rent these links for a monthly fee. The idea is since the links are on a page with incoming links and age they are more valuable. In practice, these sites have an easily identifiable high content/backlink ratio. I've read several credible sounding reports of these networks losing PR. Hopefully, the owners would notify renters when this happened, but I think the prospect of losing the revenue will make this not the case. In any case, local SEO is generally not competitive enough to justify link sources with a monthly fee. In addition, my experience with trying one for about six months showed no real advantage. So, stay away from homepage backlink networks for local SEO. (I'm reserving judgment for more competitive national terms.)

Overall, private networks are a go-to source for links prior to January of 2012, when Google decided to crack down in what appears to be a semi-manual effort that deindexed large chunks of some networks and entire networks in some case. Sites that lost incoming links in this way appeared to suffer from an anchor text link devaluation filter.

## Renting / Buying Links

Renting or buying links is a trusted strategy with SEO's. Large corporate SEO will use this strategy which they generally won't use to a great extent on a lot of the other discussed strategies due to scaling issues. There are sources that sell links on a lifetime basis that can be used for local SEO. These are usually sidebar links.

Bought or rented links will usually be priced by PageRank. This means you can get a relative value by evaluating the proposed link on a link evaluation tool like opensiteexplorer.org. I look for a good variety of incoming linking sites and also the site size. I am skeptical of any claim for a lifetime link and usually plan on an effective half-life of about four years. Unlike blog networks where a careful operator could possibly carry on a profitable operations for decades, someone selling lifetime links would eventually run out of effective space to be sold and lose any economic benefit of the site while retaining the cost.

This relative permanence would be one of the advantages of renting links, in that they would be more stable, for the reason that the operator would have an economic incentive to keep them operating.

I've achieved great #1 local ranking results without renting links. I really think it's overkill for local SEO except for possibly a hyper-competitive term like "Los Angeles Personal Injury". I'd really recommend setting up a good base of links with no renewal cost before resorting to rented links for Local SEO.

A reasonable price for a PR 3 link on a site for a year currently would be $20. This should be achievable with some shopping around. However, a really high quality PR 3 link on a related high quality functioning site with a small number of relevant outgoing links could be worth five times as much.

With the effective demise of public blog networks,

renting and buying links will become increasingly important. Try to locate links that could exist in some theoretical Google Utopia world, where people spend their spare time linking to good web content, and appear natural.

## Guest Posting and Pay Per Post

Guest posting is time tested and one of the most white hat methods for SEO. Basically, you find sites that you could write an informative post on and the owner will post it with some links. This helps the owner get free content and you get the links. Of course, this being the internet, there might be some payola involved. Ideally, according to Google, if that's the case you'll identify the post as sponsored in some way.

There are also sites where you can pay a blogger to write something about you and leave links.

Building links through traditional guest posting can involve a lot of prospecting. Certain companies in India have created a service offering guest posts and have created a very spammy situation where owners might not respond to legitimate offers from an expert writer. The best method is probably to try emailing but be prepared to actually call prospective linkees.

Overall, the occasional guest post can be worth it. I haven't used it for any of my local sites, but it does generate incredibly high quality links. In fact, the links are so high quality that it can be worthwhile to build links to those links. In addition, since these are functioning sites the link will probably stick around for a very long time and acquire quite a bit of value. Sites such as www.myblogguest.com facilitate the process of finding blogs that accept guest content.

Be careful hiring people to create guest blog posts, as a well known scam is to sell posts on blogs that are maintained specifically to sell links on. These are notably less stable than a post on a blog with a real following.

## Social Bookmarking

Social bookmarking is one of the oddest forms of linking to consider. I'd consider the links ranks under article in terms of value, but above autogenerated blog comments. A social bookmarking site is a social media site that allows people to post links to sites they've found have some value. A lot of these sites have become no-follow since they presented such an obvious target for link spam. The biggest and more prestigious sites such as Digg or Reddit might have PageRanks of 9.

It's still possible to get a do-follow link on Digg by reaching the front page. This is done by getting a certain number of bookmarks in a short quantity of time. This, along with the potential for a truly massive front page traffic burst, has spawned a certain industry of semi-professional diggers who communicate with each other to vote up articles and video content. The content usually is buzz worthy by itself and these diggers generally try to generate enough interest so that the article will encounter a cascade effect and reach the front page. The general charge for this kind of service will frequently be around a thousand dollars.

Fortunately, this is not the kind of thing that local SEO needs or requires. Plumbers in Chicago rarely generate national attention in a way that includes a website link, so you won't be competing against this in all likelihood.

Local SEO may use services that post sites to lesser sites that remain do-follow. There are a limited number of these sites so it's unlikely you can achieve your goals with social bookmarking alone. It's fairly cheap though so it's a good way to diversify your link base and it appears legitimate in a link profile analysis.

## Link Exchanges

Exchanging links with quality related sites on a resource page or site-wide blog roll style links is an old standby. I'd avoid going overboard with more than a hundred links or so due to Google warnings about doing this in excess, but it still works. You aren't limited to merely reciprocal linking but can increase the structure's complexity if you have multiple sites. Professional SEO's can do this especially well as they have a larger number of sites they are working with. You get these by old fashion pounding the pavement, prospecting through email or even phone calls.

## Developing Your Own Network

Developing your own network of sites is a technique you could consider or hire out. It's fairly involved however. You find abandoned sites with good links that are expiring and repurpose them to link to your site. You'll need to setup multiple hosting accounts and have private registration on the domains.

This technique is uniquely effective, but it's outside the scope of a simple book. You might engage an SEO to build a network for you; expect to pay about $50 or more per site plus about $30 per domain a year for maintenance. It's okay to defray costs somewhat by trading links but you want to avoid the sites having the same outgoing links since Google detects these sites, most likely by pattern matching outgoing links.

## Advanced Web and SEO Strategies

Once you've established and promoted a quality web presence it's possible to expand on your reach with strategies built on expanding the number of sites leading back to you. Having multiple sites advertising your business is not explicitly disallowed though they could be construed as landing pages, and this seems tacky. It used to be that you could establish and rank Web 2.0's; currently they all seem panda-ed and hard to rank. The only service that still works for that kind of SEO spamming is Google Plus at the moment.

There are lots of angles to take to arrive at legitimate secondary websites. A blog can be SEO'd like any other website and it's very common to have it separate from a main site. You could also have individual employees develop a blog or web presence. Certain areas such as lawyers might have distinguishable areas of practice and it looks very natural to develop sites dedicated to a specific niche.

Video is another area where there is currently a lot of opportunity. If you develop a killer video that you post on your site you can reuse that video by posting it on YouTube. The page with the video will have space for you to post a description. You can then promote the video through linkbuilding as any other website. This is great because Google seems to attempt to vary the nature of front page results so a video can potentially occupy front page results with minimal links.

## Google Places or Maps

Called Google Places or Maps, these results come from a database of local Places maintained by Google. On local searches these results can take up to half the search traffic. It's much trickier to rank these results for competitive terms but a good listing can get a great deal of traffic, especially for long-tail terms that even for local traffic you wouldn't bother building links for. It can also get traffic for when people enter in a specific term like "bankruptcy lawyer" without a local qualifier.

The good news is that the work needed to setup an effective listing is much less than SEO-ing a website for a local business. I still find Google Places to seem much like a clunky work-in-progress, but it's still better than the Bing or Yahoo products which seem to be total messes and have been marked in Beta for several years. As in SEO, it's standard practice to optimize for Google. In fact, for local map listing Bing and Yahoo haven't actually merged their systems, so there's even less volumetric reasons to optimize for them.

## Factors in Ranking a Places Page

1. Citations – A citation is a mention of the business

or place on the internet. It's basically the link for the purposes of Google Places.

2. Proximity to Search Location – Google can detect to a fairly defined area the IP address where a search is coming from. It will try to rank relevant results close to the search. Unfortunately, for searches that are outside the city it will default to the city centroid which is a location Google has determined to be the center of the city.

3. Reviews – Google seems to like businesses that have a large number of reviews. The Google Places page has reviews. If you get to 5 Google Places page reviews Google will show the star rating by the review, and this can have a very significant positive effect on site traffic.

4. Time Listing Has Existed – Google seems to trust older listings more.

5. On Site Factors – Google will determine a website associated with a Places listing. This site should have an address and number listed as well as a KML file that will show Google what location the website is attached to.

6. Links To The Google Places Page- This is widely disputed as being effective but I've seen results of other people's experiments on Xrumer blasts to people's Google Places pages. They generated significant movement.

7. Rich Text Markup on Site – Google will allow you

to mark up certain data. Putting data on your connected main website that verifies location data on your Places page seems to help, as does linking to the Places page.

## Citations

Citations are the bread and butter of ranking a Places page. You should think about citations before setting up your Places page because Google seems to scan for citations upon setting up the Places page. The more citations a site has, the higher it will rank. Google used to display a list of related sites at the bottom of a Places page. It would recalculate about once a month and the number of items on the list would change, and the ranking of the Places pages would change in response.

Unfortunately, in early 2011 Google changed format and stopped displaying this list of related sites, so it's now quite a bit harder to find out exactly what Google is counting as a citation. Unlike traditional linkbuilding, it's never been exactly clear what made Google count a citation. General rules derived from the time of openness were that well linked pages with all pertinent contact information had the greatest chance of counting as citations. Even then, just leaving your information on a page wasn't sufficient to get a citation. There seems to be some sort of algorithm Google employs to identify citations to local businesses related for determining if a site might be a directory and the relatedness of links.

The first step to building citations therefore is submission to directory sites. There are a large number of these sites, some of which share data. Certain services popped up to take advantage of this and try to offer you the ability to manage your citations all from one place. Due to widely reported reliability problems, the current best practice is to hand-submit to local directory sites. This gives you much more control over the listing as well and will give you a fighting chance if you ever change addresses.

This would obviously take you quite awhile. Fortunately, there are several services developed by internet marketers that have trained their outsourcers to do this submission. They will then send you a sheet with all the sites submitted to as well as the account login information. The cost is minimal and about a dollar each. I suggest getting the full package, which is usually about a hundred sites and may include some linking to the links the service builds. If you want to save money and do it yourself all these services will usually post their current submission list as part of their advertisement.

These directory sites usually will include a link to your website that's quite decent and very legitimate looking on the link profile.

These directory submissions will generate quite a few calls from telemarketers who throw in an "upgrade" offer along with the information verification. Just politely decline. I find a good excuse is that you have enough business and just want to be found if a customer is looking for you. You should look into portals based on traffic, and only three of these directory pages are worth looking at (YellowPages, Yellowbook, and Superpages).

## Setting Up A Google Places Page Is Fairly Easy.

The first and most important step is to make sure you don't have a Google Places page already. Google scans many other directory sites and will create a Places page in many instances. This is an unclaimed page; unclaimed pages can attract citations like any other pages. In addition, it's not unheard of for marketing companies to hijack these listings for the leads or to ransom them. It can be very hard to kill these auto-created Google Places pages unless you can determine the data source Google is using to create it. If you get multiple pages Google can potentially split the citations between them and make ranking very difficult or, in some cases, impossible. Go to Google Maps and enter your address, business name, and phone number, and make sure for each you don't have an entry. It can also pay to check old addresses.

You will need to upload five videos off YouTube and ten pictures that you can upload to Google. When you upload the videos to YouTube make sure your description contains all the information constituting a citation.

You may be able to title the Google Places page. Keywords in the title can make it rank better, but can also lead to lower ranking for stuffing. It needs to be natural and appear consistent. So, add the words Team or Group to the description if you are doing something like "City + keyword" for the title. It's also safest if the title appears on your website.

There are five category listings you can use. Google has a number of preset categories it will suggest for you, and you can enter custom categories if nothing fits. This used to be an opportunity for keyword stuffing but that can now result in the listing not showing.

Once you have entered everything, Google will

require you to verify the listing. The two options are phone and postcard verification. Some industries like locksmiths might require postcard verification due to a high fraud possibility.

Google will then take up to about a day to display changes or a new listing.

Monitoring progress on a Google Places page can be very slow. Google updates the citations monthly and it can take a long time to get credit for what you've done. You can check the traffic by logging back into the same account you setup Google Places in. It's unlikely to be much until it's gaining a top seven result.

## Pay Per Click

Pay Per Click (PPC) or the sponsored results is how you get that fabled number #1 result in Google overnight. I'm currently not blown away with the profit potential for Pay Per Click on local results. Unfortunately, PPC doesn't offer the same ROI as SEO and in competitive niches Pay Per Click delivers leads at around 50% of a sale's gross.

This might seem unnatural as to why would anyone bid the price up to such unsustainable levels. The easy explanation is a current bubble in venture capital funding companies that purport to offer expertise in managing a Pay Per Click campaign. These companies hire banks of aggressive cold callers who they can run at a loss while trying to show the growth needed to go public. Some of these companies won't even disclose their fees, claiming that it's part of a difficult to explain algorithm, but generally can run over half the ad spend. I'm pretty sure this bubble will eventually burst when they've exhausted the pool of business owners who'll give it a go. For now though, PPC isn't the road to riches unless you're in a niche with a good number of searches and low competition.

Once you have a good website it can be worthwhile to try a PPC campaign. It's easy enough to try managing yourself or you can usually outsource it for around 20% of the ad-spend, with a $200 minimum. Elance can generate some very credible providers. I'll go over the basics of setting up and how to run a local Google PPC campaign.

If you get a good Pay Per Click campaign established, you can copy the ads over to Yahoo and Bing and get a campaign going there too.

The key rules for Local PPC -

1. The most valuable hours will be the hours you can service the call and answer the lead.
2. Remember to set the geotargeting.
3. Limit your results to Google Search results.

PPC is a subject covered much more easily in a video, so visit my site http://www.critwit.com for a brief training video on the subject.

## Google Adwords Express

Formerly called Google Boost, this is a product offered by Google with the idea of offering local businesses an easy to understand alternative to Adwords. The product essentially promotes a Google Places profile. As an advantage to Adwords it would also show the star ranking on the ad. This would hopefully increase your quality score and CTR.

Unfortunately, in practice using the product is a complete and money draining waste of time. In an effort to simplify the product Google took away a number of targeting options. You can't pick or exclude keywords so you're going to be spending money on potential renters if you're a real estate agent who doesn't do that and similar situations will occur across virtually all industries. In addition, you can't target the time of day. The best leads are during the day when the lead can communicate immediately, has a fresh need and has not shopped around. Google Adwords Express won't let you do this. It also apparently uses the same quality score for bid pricing as regular Adwords which, since you're not allowed to target anything, means that you're going to paying way too much.

Overall, while some super low competition niches like dog walkers might find this profitable, it's going to be a money-loser for competitive niches.

# Competitiveness of Niches

Local SEO is generally not competitive unless a competent SEO has been involved with a niche at some point. It's fairly easy to check the number of links for the top sites in www.opensiteexplorer and I find this generally accurate for difficulty to rank since link building is the critical factor for deciding between results.

If you spend hours and hours analyzing results you'll find that the competitiveness closely follows the categories noted for spending money on local advertising with big ticket items. I'd visualize it like this. Competition is higher in the West Coast. Generally, most terms I search in Las Vegas for example are more competitive than in New York. The most competitive term I ever looked at for local search was Los Angeles Personal Injury.

## High Competition

Bankruptcy, Family Law, and Personal Injury Law – The big consumer big spender YellowPage categories are also by far the most difficult to rank for Local SEO.

Real Estate – With most web searches being local, ranking for real estate terms can be a challenge.

## Medium Competition

These are areas that are frequent targets of SEO and have a tendency to gather a small number of aged links naturally; more competition in a major city than can fit in the top 10 results and have portal sites.

> General Practice Dentistry.
> Plastic Surgery.
> Home Improvement, Plumbing, Electrical, Granite.
> Mortgage Brokers – These have a lot of PPC competition nationally but the local organics seem doable.
> Local SEO.

## Low Competition

Everything Else.

Another way is to judge by the number of linking sites on www.opensiteexplorer.org.
I use the following general rule.

Under 20 linking sites – Very Low Competition

20-50 Low Competitions
50-200 Medium Competition
200-500 High Competitions
500+ Very High Competition

Any query can be competitive for the spots that are being actively promoted.

## Creating an SEO Plan

Once you have your site up and finished then you can start building links to it. It's hard to say exactly what your plan should be. I'd start with local directory submissions since these will help both your site and Places page. These can also be started before the site itself is fully done. Regular directory submissions are a good next step but require a finished site. Afterwards, I'd plan to spend a little time or money every two weeks or so to build some links. It's important not to be in a hurry. Getting a really good and responsive site can take up to two years, though I've had great results in low competition niches in three months.

Your aim is to be the top result. Optify released a study showing that the top three results achieved over 50% of the clicks with the first result receiving several times the second. Anyone who aims for less than #1 in local is whistling in the wind.

## Measuring SEO Results

The ultimate measure of SEO results is conversions. However, if you are getting significant traffic then measuring results in terms of traffic is a necessary metric. Traffic is not all the same however, so you need to measure by source and query. If you are getting traffic that logically should be converting it can be a good time to get a second look at your site for potential problems. If the traffic is coming from images or out of area queries then it wouldn't make sense for it to convert. Blogs are a usual culprit, generating great traffic that doesn't convert locally.

# The Other Guys
## Non-Search Ways To Promote Your Business

### The Local Celebrity Plan

The local celebrity plan can work for certain industries. I semi-tried this as a divorce lawyer in Memphis with a dining and review blog that had some following, but never got any significant business from it. However, I know of a realtor who's gotten quite a bit of business with the same tactic.

This strategy is especially suited for high use personal services. I recommend it especially for attractive women who will find celebrity easier to gain.

Basically, you try to become a resource for things to do around your town. This is fun as it provides an excuse for dining out and such. There's actually a need for this and popular local blogs can get a real readership usually combined with a good social media presence. Since blogs can usually auto-update social media platforms it's easy to update whatever platforms make sense.

## Evaluating Portals

There's a booming industry of portals out there. They seek to monetize themselves in various ways. Sites such as Yelp, Avvo (Lawyer Specific), Zillow (Real Estate), and an innumerable number of others attempt to be an online YellowPages, selling advertising and placement . Others such as ServiceMagic and the lawyer specific Total Network sell leads to specific customers. Then there are mixed approaches such as LegalMatch.

It's fairly easy to evaluate the lead sellers. Take your cost per lead divided by your expected closing rate to come up with a cost per customer. Since you know your businesses costs and accounting percentages you get a rough sense of your income from these methods. Lead sellers will often bill the limited number of marketing partners in an area as some sort of quality check, possibly giving you slightly greater creditability. Some companies will offer non-exclusive leads which should figure into your analysis. These shared leads can be a good deal if you're especially responsive or the lead generator lacks another customer in the area.

Lead sellers also typically have much shorter contractual commitment than directories, so you can test out your assumptions. Also, discount expected closing rates the salesman suggests by at least 50%. Typically your closing rate will be lower than with leads generated off your own websites, but you'll find a slightly higher level of client contacting you and giving you a chance to close with some lead sellers. While practicing law I never encountered a lead seller that wasn't willing to give a significant discount over the initial quote. The best strategy is to seem interested and tell them to check back in a week or two.

Many lead sellers will generate their traffic through PPC. This is reasonable but can lead to conflicts of interest like aggressive bidding in the middle of the night, when local businesses leads during daylight hours are far more valuable. I'd prefer to see strong SEO results and good sites as proposed to lead sources.

Directories can be much more difficult to evaluate. The one thing you almost should never be wowed by is the design of the website. Volume of usage is the most important and relevant criteria. For YellowPage sites I'd stick to sites with a print directory in your area. Most directories offer a free listing that will help your SEO and other efforts. The big three online YellowPages are

Superpages.com, YellowPages.com, and Yellowbook.com according to Comscore, and I wouldn't do any advertising on a internet YellowPage site except those three since they each achieve several times the volume of sites out of the top three. You'll probably want to stay away from enhanced listings in any directory until you've thoroughly explored options with your own website and Pay Per Click.

I'm not a big fan of portal sites. I rarely hear of people getting a good ROI as much as I hear how nice the cute rep was. They're good in concept but, like Pay Per Click, portals have a large amount of venture capital being invested, so they can run the sales reps at a loss to get good revenue growth and not worry about customer retention.

## QR Codes

A QR code is a two dimensional bar code created in 1994 to aid in inventory tracking in the automotive industry. See below for an example which leads to my website.

These have now become all the rage, being posted on everything from real estate yard signs to rooftops. The basic idea is that these codes will contain instructions that when read by a reader (usually on a smartphone) will perform an action such as going to a webpage, joining a SMS/text service, downloading a virtual business card, or playing a YouTube video.

It's an interesting concept but overplayed as a brilliant idea. It is definitely something a marketer should be aware of though. Putting QR codes on menus to sign up for Twitter or an SMS service is the best idea I've heard. In addition, it's usually possible to capture the phone number of a QR code user for follow-up which would be useful when someone reads a real estate sign. Currently, the evidence suggests that most people don't actually know what these are and don't use them. I'd really think about them in more high tech areas like San Francisco.

## SMS

Short message service or text messaging can be an extremely effective form of advertising to frequently use for local businesses. How it works is that basically, someone texts a signup code specific to your establishment to a service providers number. Through this provider you can send short messages to customers. Restaurants can send out last minute specials on slow nights or bars could text quick enticing reports about how P-Diddy just walked in the door.

The key to these service is getting signups. Usually you'll have to offer an immediately useable discount for subscribing to the service.

SMS marketing is roughly equivalent to Twitter marketing but with a greater usage. Receivers will have to pay their text fees. Signing up to an SMS service should be roughly sixty dollars a month with a set allowance of texts.

## Social Media

Social media is all the rage, with interesting products coming out all the time for gurus to market. It's also probably the least complicated of all avenues to understand. Social media is a media that offers the possibility for interaction between the users. This was difficult before the internet era, though bulletin boards and the town square offer some interesting parallels.

If I have a negative stance towards social media, it's because of some issues I frequently see. Social media requires the highest time investment from someone knowledgeable about the day to day business operations. This point is often neglected by social media gurus. While we're on the guru subject, I think it's frequently forgotten how new social media really is. Twitter was established in 2006, so it's going to be hard for someone to establish themselves as an expert.

Also, I see social media as much more fragmented then the popular norm. While there are connections between Facebook/Twitter, Twitter/Foursquare, etc., I don't see these interactions as having any more or less complexity then the interactions between print ads/Twitter. While social media forums do tend to lend themselves to having a company related principal conducting the various feeds, on a strategic level they need to fit into a marketing plan as though they were all independent portals and strategies. This also counteracts the jargon based tendency to quote figures for social media that sound impressive, but then you figure out that Facebook alone will account for 60-80% of statistics.

It also really seems as though social media usage

figures can be greatly exaggerated. Part of this is due to the number of abandoned accounts, but a fair bit of fake active users exist as internet marketers create fake robotic personas that simulate actual people for SEO purposes. This is especially true in my view for Twitter, whereas Facebook is really good at cracking down on fake accounts. I also feel as though people don't typically mention their local businesses on social media in a positive manner, though location-based check-in is a trend that may change this.

Social media really shines in national level networking. For local it's going to be the best strategy for high frequency fun venues such as restaurants, farmers markets, and bands. These kinds of businesses will find it easiest to get followers since they can offer genuinely needed information. One of the most frequently used application success stories is food trucks, whose mobile nature makes their location inherently valuable. Word of mouth is undeniably important, but it's difficult to market local businesses using social media due to infrequency of use for many local businesses such as lawyers or realtors and the inherently smaller number of people involved in niche markets.

It's critically important to be aware of social media

for any local business for a different reason than business promotion. In the event of negative experiences, gripes and complaints can get posted very quickly to social media outlets and stick in people's minds.

In short, a social media strategy is this: Create a stream of content on these sites and then get followers.

## Stream of Content

The stream of content doesn't need to be deep and in fact it shouldn't be. The number one mistake in social media marketing is excessive updates. Social media users will find that your feed dilutes the experience and will delete you. In no case would I post more than one update a day except in very special circumstances, such as on the weekend for popular bars and clubs *e.g.* (The crazy tropical's Bunga-Bunga part tonight will be super awesome with hot chicks and cheap drinks!!) then (Bunga-Bunga's turning into the hottest party of the year!). Boring businesses like lawyers and plumbers should try to keep it to once per week.

Good content is daily specials, quick tips, and limited time offers. You can also post images to recent work, and before and after photos. Twitter has services that will generate a special shortened link to put into tweets.

The second mistake in social media is not updating often enough. If you never update your feed, it will become irrelevant.

## Getting Followers

Getting followers is the hardest part of social media. The most common strategy is to put your Facebook page and Twitter ID on all your marketing material. You can also use a QR code on the marketing material.

A very popular technique is to follow or friend people and hope they follow you back. This works best for attractive women or businesses that can make an attractive woman a spokesperson for their business. I'd note that most realtors promoting a social media course or product for other realtors I've received seemed to be attractive women.

## Major Categories of Social Networking

Social Networking sites function primarily as a way for people to connect. The big one is Facebook but there is also LinkedIn with a business focus, and Google is launching an attempt called Google+. Twitter is somewhat unique and lets people communicate via 140 character messages called tweets. There is also location-based social media that let people share check-ins at real world locations with their connections utilizing a smartphone. Examples are Foursquare and a service called Gowala. The functionality of these sites has been essentially duplicated as a sub-feature of Facebook and Yelp and personally I believe that these sites are going to be defunct soon.

## Facebook

Facebook, established in 2004, is the largest social media site and currently the most popular website in the world. It has a number of features that make it a useful avenue for marketing some local businesses.

### Facebook PPC

Facebook has a very neat Pay Per Click ad feature that uses its users data to create hyper-targeted ads.

You can aim by interests, employer, age, or even relationship status. It's possible to hyper-target to even target one person. A very neat feature is the ability to target friends of certain individuals. If you provide a personalized service such as realtor or lawyer you could advertise just to your Facebook social circle, which should contain lots of people who may vaguely recognize you but don't really think of you in connection to the services you provide.

Facebook PPC generally gets a fairly low click through rate so if you're trying to raise brand awareness you might want to use the Cost Per Thousand or CPM option they have available. It works much in the same way as regular Pay Per Click and you'll need to think of a short catchy tag line. You also have the ability to put a small picture in the ad, which is an absolute must. You can also offer the option in the ad of liking your business page.

## Business Pages

Facebook offers an option of a Facebook specific business page. They can range from a fairly stock look to hiring a designer to make a catchy one. You can get a fixed URL once you reach 25 fans. You can also buy fans off Fiverr and other services to reach the 25 or acquire social proof to make it look like your business is popular.

There are also attractive women on Fiverr who'll pretend to be in a relationship with someone for a week who you could probably hire to comment and act interested on your fanpage to create a buzz.

The main point of getting a vibrant Facebook page is to be able to send out profile updates that will go to your followers. Certain businesses will benefit even more though if they offer events, as events are the killer Facebook application for the young professional with a good number using it to organize their calendar. The newsfeed application is frequently hidden but events will be checked.

Facebook pages frequently come up as citations for Google Places so be sure to have one even if it's just basic with a filled out profile, phone, website, and address. Getting a good number of real Facebook likes can help with Bing search results, as a logged in user will see friends who Facebook-like search results, increasing their click through rate.

Location Based

Location based services such as Foursquare and Facebook check-in offer opportunities for people to share their locations and goings on.

## Twitter

Twitter is a social network that limits its users to 140 character messages or tweets. Twitter's less personal short messages have led to a much different and more impersonal feel than Facebook. People can follow others. Celebrities use Twitter to communicate with their fans.

I'm not a fan of Twitter for most local businesses. If you keep up a blog you can usually enable it to tweet the title of your posts which won't hurt. Restaurants might be able to get something going but I'd lean more towards text/SMS marketing first. I can see creative local applications like a 'deal of the week' stream for real estate. Twitter will be more relevant in areas with a large young tech-savvy population.

## Groupon, Living Social, etc.

A very interesting concept has arisen recently called the daily deal site or Groupon. The idea is basically a service (in Groupon's case a website/email marketing list) that offers regular periodic goods packages from local merchants. The value of this stream is sufficient to induce a group of loyal followers.

Businesses offer these deals through the service and split the payment. The deal is typically basically a gift certificate at half price, though some merchants will offer a specific item or service. There will frequently also be a social aspect to the service such as receiving a free deal if a certain number of your friends signup due to sharing, or in Groupon's case, requiring a minimum number of signups before the deal is issued.

Central to evaluating this idea is the one of Lifetime Customer Value. Most businesses will be losing money on the payment they receive from the deal site. Typically these sites will take around half the payment. The idea is that you will gain a number of regular customers.

So, if you're a restaurant (the most popular deal) and you sell 20 units of food for 10$ and you sell a 1000 deals, you'll get a payment of 5000$. Then you'll be expected to honor those 1000 deals, though some won't show.

If your food cost is 7$ and you have slack

capacity and aren't bumping any full pays then you're going be losing 2000$ on the deal. What you're hoping for of course is that either they'll buy additional food on the visit, become repeat customers, or recommend you to someone else.

Very few of these sites will let you limit the number of deals sold and they're all known for not remembering to set limits, even if they've agreed to. There are numerous cases of people crediting daily deal sites for bankrupting their company.

Overall, use this strategy with caution and make sure that you have rock solid customer retention strategies in place before starting to maximize your return on investment.

## Email

Email is one of the most powerful tools in the marketing world. Local is no exception, but it's more of a lead follow-up tool. Some industries might be able to use unsolicited emails to groups that they particularly select for, like home inspectors and realtors. I would be very careful with unsolicited emails. Local operates in a small circle so more than once every six or twelve months and you could acquire a bad reputation.

Email is also covered by specific laws created to fight email spam. Spam is the bulk sending of unsolicited messages though the term has been widened to include the sending of content for the exclusive purpose of leaving a link. Passed in 2005, the CAN SPAM law only covers currently email messages and not blog and forum spamming (though there's a possibility that a forum's private message system would be covered, and there are also some torts that could possibly cover the behavior).

In order to comply with Can-Spam as of writing (and it does change) you'll need to provide an opt-out mechanism and put your physical name and address in the message.

The best use for email is for communicating with individuals who've already expressed an interest in your services, or past customers. Some services such as restaurant/venues and realtors have natural reasons for higher frequency contact. As a general rule for lawyers, mortgage brokers, and any business without a good reason for more frequent contact, I'd say bi-monthly is a good contact frequency.

There are two methods I've seen to be effective. A newsletter is the most traditional form. The most effective newsletters I've heard of tend to be short (2 paragraphs max) with links to click to for further information. These links can lead your own content on a blog or to other content. I'd suggest a mix is best since it makes the message seem less commercial.

Your newsletter doesn't necessarily need to be tied directly to your industry. Some plumbing companies in my area are known for general newsletters with punch recipes and other fun content. Certain industries such as law that score very low on the fun index should keep coverage of their own area to a minimum (this isn't applicable if trying to network with other related professionals for referrals, obviously).

The other really effective technique is a 'just checking in' email. For example:

Dear Potential Customer,

We were happy to have provided you with information about your previous query. We thought it would be a good idea to check in and see if you needed any further information or help.

Very Truly Yours,

Local Small Business

There are a variety of software programs such as 'constant contact' that you can load email addresses into to mass send, and which also have an unsubscribe feature to keep Can-Spam violations to a minimum. These programs will also usually have an ability to report statistics on open rate and how many people unsubscribe. The best time to send emails is either early morning or late afternoon. Outlook has a scheduling feature, but I found that too many entries make the program unstable.

A technique related to email is offering a course or ebook that people can get in exchange for signing up for your newsletter. This technique is best for non-local marketing. Most local businesses want to encourage contact as fast as possible with a salesperson. A responder series makes it slightly more difficult to immediately contact potential clients.

## Events

Events are a powerful form of marketing for local businesses. Quiz nights, receptions, and other draws can act as a catalyst for great local branding. Filling your schedule is a killer app for a lot of social media users so offering a good event schedule can generate good interactions. Charities will run a lot of fundraisers at near breakeven after staff costs just for this reason. Facebook gives a very good placement to event invitations and many people use it as their major social event calendar.

## Traditional Media Outlets

I'd say print media publications, YellowPages, radio and television constitute the major avenues of traditional media outlets. These avenues, as well as generating leads by themselves, can be used to drive traffic towards your website or social media channels. The availability of cost effective number tracking and traffic techniques makes traditional media more quantifiable than ever. You can put a specific URL for print ads or achieve an approximate track by seeing an increase in type-in traffic.

## YellowPages/Yellowbook

These still have a large following in some circles and an older demographic. In addition, they tend to better organized than the internet in some local areas. Certain service businesses may be benefit from these outlets. My experience was excellent one year and money losing the next in my law practice. Thoughtfully, the year with the largest ad had the smallest results. It's worth giving it a try for a year for established businesses but should be tracked carefully. I saw a significant amount of type-in traffic on my website when I started running a Yellowbook ad, so definitely make sure your ad includes your site and also your social media channels if they're impressive.

## Print Media

The key to evaluating print media is demographics. Alternative weeklies can have very high readership. I pulled enough cases to at least pay for my ads when I advertised in the local alternative paper's classified. It also generated an impressive brand awareness as in "your that lawyer who advertises in the flyer" which helped in closing deals.

I also know of some serious success cases involving print media in smaller markets. Some tips for print media are that you'll need to advertise for awhile. It can take six months to start to see results. It's really a brand awareness type strategy.

There are a number of specialty giveaway

publications that I'd be careful of unless they have a very long track record. They are usually run by serial entrepreneurs who have a bad habit of not selling enough ads to go to publication but using the ad sales as they come in to meet daily living expenses.

## Radio and Television

Radio and television are fairly similar to print media. They probably have a slightly shorter testing period. Radio and TV both have outlet level demographic considerations. A particularly intriguing possibility for businesses is that some (usually AM) stations may offer you the possibility to host you own show for a set fee. There are certain service businesses where the owner has built up a following simply by having their own local radio show.

## Phone Calls

It's fairly accepted among realtors that if you're not picking up the phone and calling people you're not going to be doing any business. It's easy to rely on webcentric crutches as a substitute for personal contact, but every business needs to ask itself if there is any way to be contacting former clients and regulars. Phone calls are cheap and even having a hostess call past clients during slack time might generate extra business.

From working legal leads I can say that up to half the value of a lead may be tied into quality follow-up and contacts. In addition, an occasional "how are you doing" from any service provider, even a plumbing company, might generate new business.

## Direct Mail

Direct mail is the ancestor of email marketing. It's fallen off quite a bit in the internet era, but the saturation effect of nearly-free email has meant that it can still be a very effective medium. The higher cost of mail means that you're competing with far fewer advertisers. In addition, the increasing sophistication of data providers means that you can purchase extremely targeted lists by income, age, or a large number of credit based selects.

It's also a potent tool for customer retention with the infamous birthday club being a mainstay of restaurant marketing.

Good resources for exploring direct mail are any

book by Dan Kennedy, and www.bestratereferrals.com is a good source for credit bureau leads that you can select for many factors.

# Putting It All Together and Advanced Topics

## Outsourcing

Outsourcing your own SEO, PPC, or website design directly is a tricky thing. I've pulled great graphic design, content, and good tech support off of www.Odesk.com and www.Elance.com but the repetitive and low skill nature of most SEO tasks makes it difficult to find good, reliable providers. You can work around this problem by offering larger job sizes, but most local businesses aren't going to need the quantity of services necessary to get reliable help. I'd guess the sweet spot to get the professional providers is around $250.

Elance offers a feature to highlight your job for $15 which will get you a great deal of bids. Providers on Elance normally have a set number of times they can bid depending on their membership plan. A featured job usually won't count against them. The limited number of bids on Elance is an advantage of their platform as you get fewer template bids that don't fit what you're asking for, and you can get great information and ideas of what you want to ask for.

It's best to spec out a request for bids on any freelance site to the most detailed and specific extent possible. It's amazing the ways contractors can mess things up in ways you've never contemplated, from not capitalizing any words to an inability to use paragraphs. Things like relevant, on point blog commenting I've found impossible to outsource, since contractors will do the bare minimum that can be considered job completion. It's also impossible to pay for quality. I've even found that offering bonuses for good work doesn't help either.

A good trick on either site is to search for similar jobs and use those descriptions as a template of what to start from.

I personally tend to use Odesk for content much more as the prices tend to be much lower. The Philippines has a rich English language tradition and I've found a lot of good writers come from there. Design and other services, well, I've found Elance to be the better source.

On the feedback watch for longer ratings as more reliable. Most systems let contractors rate the job providers as well so there's a tendency to be very kind towards the more inept ones.

Forums such as www.warriorforum.com and www.trafficplanet.com have services sections that can have good providers for article writing and various types of directory submissions. It's safest to pick providers with fairly long running posts with responses, but it's always tricky using these services. One favorite trick is to check the post history of the thread poster.

## Lead Handling

It's the pet peeve of virtually all internet marketing consultants and also one of the most valid. Particularly in the legal field, it's amazing how often a firm spending a million dollars a year on advertising will have the phone answered by a slightly hostile receptionist who has major cigarette voice with a quick "law office" without even a "How can I help you?"

I answered my own phone for a good percentage

of my practice and I think all business owners should make an effort to answer the phone at least a certain percentage of the time. It's a great way to get a first hand impression of the quality of leads you're getting, what your customers concerns are, and how to close sales. This will enable you to supervise and direct the initial intake employees earlier.

If your business or time commitments preclude phone screening there are options covered under tracking that will allow you to record incoming calls for review.

Internet leads are notorious for being information shoppers as well so you'll need to be prepared for the occasional follow-up call and long lead conversions. I've had people I'd talked to well over a year ago come back and hire me. For real estate there's a noted broker in Florida named Mitch Ribak who's developed an entire system for follow-up called 100 MPH marketing, that every agent thinking of using internet leads should use and I'd recommend it to any business as a great foundation in lead management. It also will dispel any notion that simply having great marketing will suffice.

However, don't be too quick to blame lead handling or accept an internet consultant's explanation that you're just blowing all the good leads he's sending.

Lead quality and volume are important. You'll never get 100% conversion. Legal leads run around 10% with good follow-up and the top realtor I'm aware of in internet leads has figures under 5% with real estate conversion (most realtors convert internet leads less than 1% of the time, and 2% is decent).

## Reputation Management

Reputation management is one of the hottest new products being offered and it's an advanced strategy. Basically, internet reputation management seeks to ensure that when someone searches for you or your business, they find complimentary material and reviews.

This generally involves SEO on the most positive sites to ensure that they come up first. So, a politician would have links built to articles on a policy initiative until it overwhelms, say, a sexual harassment story. Similarly, if someone built a "yousuck.com" targeting your business you would link-build to articles and directories already close to start ranking for your name. In extreme cases you might need to make some charitable donations with a deal that a brief article goes into the charities site that you could target (charities usually have great sites.) You might also need to build ancillary sites such as blogs and specialty service focused sites. This is obviously a great business to be in because you'll be performing SEO on a large number of sites, however typically for a local business you won't be looking at really competitive space and applicable terms so don't get ripped off.

The other major reputation management activity is review management. In most cases, the company will seek to push reviews down the page. In some cases it may be possible to get your own customers to write enough reviews to accomplish this (see review getting). In all likelihood though a review management company will manufacture the reviews to accomplish this in a steady erratic pattern, in order to escape filters looking for suspicious reviews (such as 20 left in a 2 hour increment by the same computer). Usually, these companies will have aged accounts that they can use for this. They can also use a technology called proxies that mask which computer the review is placed from. They also might find them on Fiverr which has an ample selection of service providers to leave fake reviews. Posting fake reviews is fairly standard in internet marketing and technically a violation punishable by the FTC with sizeable fines. To my mind most firms hire reputation management companies to achieve plausible deniability. It may be possible in some cases to get sites to remove reviews, either by a complaint that the reviews were published by a competitor or with the fact that they are irrelevant. I've also heard of threatening legal action occasionally working but as a general rule it is extremely expensive and uncertain.

To be honest this is an area that is rapidly getting out of control. I personally don't provide review management but I can see aggressive action almost being necessary to survive for some businesses. I can also see a future where reviews become almost useless as competitors will seek to skewer each other.

The best defense is outstanding customer service and being nice to competitors. However, I don't think any business can be 100% all the time and certain business like legal services and landlording are going to get bad reviews as a matter of course.

Sites typically offer owners the opportunity to respond to reviews and you should be doing this routinely. The key is to apologize and promise to review your procedures for higher frequency businesses.

# Ways to Charge for SEO and Google Places Consulting

## Site Lease

Since ranking a site takes so long, sometimes an SEO consultant will develop the site and then seek to rent it out on a month-to-month basis. The SEO consultant will usually own the attached phone number and forward it to the business. This is a great method although of limited availability since it requires investment on the part of the consultant. The site could be rented based on calls and leads generated or on a flat monthly fee.

In either case you should be able to look at a track record of traffic and calls. This takes much of the guesswork and risk related to the inherent sketchiness of many SEO salespeople out of the equation. It's also great for the SEO since the product is predefined and they don't have to worry about handholding.

If you can find someone who does this, if they don't have a pre-done site it's possible they would start development work after a sincere expression of interest from you.

## Setup + Monthly Charge

This is the most popular form of SEO contract. The SEO gets a monthly fee to perform "SEO services" for a number of keywords. In most cases there isn't even a predefined list of services that must be performed in a certain order. This to me seems like a recipe for dissatisfaction. It's like hiring someone to write a book for a monthly fee with no deadline. It's somewhat better if there is a set number of links that will be built, though I've rarely seen a package I would ever buy.

With the increased emphasis on extremely private networks, it makes sense now to have some maintenance element.

## Hybrid Flat Fee Method/How I Do It

My favorite method, when I'm not pre-doing sites for lease, is to pick the top five most competitive keywords. I usually then come up with a flat fee for establishing a #1 result for one of the keywords and #1-3 for the rest. I charge up to half as an upfront fee for setup of the basic directory links and Google Places. I don't do local SEO without Google Places since they are so interconnected.

Next, I have progress payments at all terms on page 1, then all terms in the top 5 results and then the contract result maintained for a month. I then charge a continued retainer and non complete fee of 15% of the contract price yearly as long as top #3 results are maintained. I might charge 25% yearly to continue ranking for other terms.

Most SEO consultants who are confident of their ranking abilities should agree to some variation above for local SEO terms.

Traffic Increase

Charging for traffic increase is another method. It's not an overly popular for local SEO and is prone to manipulation. For example, listing a large number of images on a website or blogging can lead to a lot of traffic from Google Image results that isn't targeted. In addition, even a little linkbuilding on a site without any at all can lead to impressive gains. It is a good factor to keep in mind, potentially for performance bonuses.

# Factors In Hiring An SEO/Marketing Consultant

1. References – It's difficult to evaluate references in this day and age. Really good salespeople can have an almost supernatural ability to have some happy clients no matter what they charge. In addition, there might be a preexisting relationship where the SEO consultant knew them. It's also possible that the reference was in a particularly good undiscovered niche with little competition.

2. Results - Fortunately, unlike with certain field like financial advising, it's fairly easy to see an SEO's results. It's difficult to evaluate this for the layperson. Ideally you'd like to see #1 results for either the main legal niches (bankruptcy, personal injury, divorce) or real estate for major metros. This should be for core terms such as (city service) not (service in city) or a modifier such as (good city service).

3. Contract Terms and Incentives - Is the SEO

willing to tie a substantial portion of compensation to results either in terms of rankings or traffic? As stated before, I think a monthly fee is ridiculous for most SEO projects unless you are buying a quantified number of links.

4. Projects – Most competent SEO's will be working on ranking their own websites, either as future rentals or internet marketing projects. They are confident of generating a positive ROI.

5. Proposed Keywords - Stay away from SEO's who want to target longer tail phrases without going for the key terms. Local has such low search volumes that this is not a good strategy.

6. Industry Familiarity – This is of moderate importance. The tools and techniques are very similar throughout industries. It is helpful to have worked with one similar client before since content writing is one of the biggest parts of SEO. Niche specialization is widely used as a marketing technique in the SEO field.

7. Holistic Approach – A good internet marketer will evaluate your business and goals and be willing to recommend services and products even if they

are outside their production. I would stay away from anyone not seriously considering social media outlets for a bar and be extremely wary of someone pushing social media for a law firm unless every other outlet was well covered.

8. Pooh–poohing Linkbuilding - Linkbuilding is the heart of Google SEO. Other factors are of course important and at the end of the day it's about conversions. Anyone with half a brain will know this. Certain marketers like to downplay linkbuilding by pointing out the obvious and leading potential clients away from the highest work/cost part of the function to perform. It typically takes half an hour to tweak a couple pages of content and tags whereas linkbuilding requires a substantial time and monetary expenditure. Stay away from anyone who denigrates linkbuilding.

9. Background – For local there are three primary backgrounds that people tend to enter from. Website designer - Typically this is bad, as website designers primarily are artists working on a per-project basis. Internet marketing and SEO in particular can take years to fine tune a correct strategy. A lot of them are charging several hundred dollars a month to change title tags.

Some programmers do SEO and are similar to web designers but usually have better results. Marketer/Get Rich Quick Person - This person has been sloshing about on the internet and happened upon forums with how-to guides on how to make money promoting local businesses. These are probably a better option than web designers since they tend to be result oriented. Former local business owner - I'll admit I'm biased toward this group since I'm included. These people tend to have been shocked at a price quote from a telemarketer while simultaneously skeptical of promised results. Typically after several years of promoting their own sites they decide they like marketing better than running their own businesses. This can be a good fit as they tend to have multiyear experience ranking sites, have experience in outsourcing services they don't perform at wholesale rates, and understand the small business.

## Saving Cash

Internet consultants can be very pricey. It can be tempting to do it yourself. Generally, the idea with do it yourself is to find areas where you can trade your time for the time of someone who might be faster but who can give you the same quality.

The biggest and most obvious area for most people is writing the website copy. It's actually hard for anyone else to capture a good personal feel. You might need to hire someone else to polish it off, but having something to go on will significantly decrease the time a copywriter should need to spend on your project.

Creating blog entries and social media content doesn't even really require polishing, but it helps. Generally, the rule is to get it out and published.

SEO and link building can be done by yourself. It mainly takes time. Local is a good place to learn SEO since the guiding principal of local link building is to go slowly.

The hardest and most necessary thing to outsource is graphic design. You can find excellent designers off the outsourcing sites at a very reasonable cost. Weebly has in-house designers that can do very good designs for, the last time I checked, 500$.

## How You're Going to Get Ripped Off

Being a small business owner you're going to get called by hordes of slick convincing salespeople selling products, services and subscriptions that can seem very convincing. They use some slick techniques that if you're consciously aware of can help you fend off that feeling of urgency good salespeople can create, and that can make you adopt suboptimal decision making.

The number one trick that can mess with your mind is confidence. Good salespeople will adopt a position that the product they're selling is the absolute best and will deliver. For most marketing products, once you understand them, this a fallacy. Virtually every product in the marketing arena involves a high level of risk (is this the right radio channel?) or is a subject to a great deal of uncertainty (SEO). Confidence is especially dangerous in the modern world since due to Darwinian selection previously false confidence would have been eliminated from the gene pool, but due to the comfy and forgiving nature of the modern world it's very difficult to suffer serious consequences of overconfidence. So, we tend to accord people portraying high confidence a high degree of presumed competence.

The related trick of undermining your confidence is another big one. A designer looks at your site and calls you up. You say you're happy with it. The designer gives a lukewarm passive aggressive response such as "I guess it's functional." This technique's effectiveness comes from undermining your confidence in a needed solution. Sales is usually a numbers game of looking for people with a need, and by undermining your confidence they're getting you to reject a solution that you've already adopted. This is much faster than looking for someone who doesn't have a need.

The second big technique is building rapport. This is accomplished by asking rhetorical questions with an obvious answer such as "you could use an additional 5-15 cases per month, right?" The best defense I've found is to agree with this but be a little hostile, at least in the back of your mind, to prevent falling for this technique.

Arguing based on logic not backed up by testing or facts. This is the classic "Google is smart" or "bigger ads are better" argument. It sounds good and respectable, but without experience and testing it's really just blowing smoke.

The strawman argument. This is creating a problem when there are none. This is the classic no hat argument of "you don't want to get penalized by Google do you?" when faced with a site getting no appreciable search traffic a month. It's not really an issue since you're not getting any business anyway, but it sounds bad.

Value attributions. This one is tricky. It's been proven time and time again that people relate price to value. The shopkeeper who can't sell some jewelry and accidentally marks it up to find it all gone has become a near urban legend. It's not like that in marketing. Price has very little relation to value. There's a frightening number of people making a good living taking a 5$ automated linkbuilding package off Fiverr and repackaging it on other sites with a fancy sales letter for 10-100x the amount. My piece of wisdom is to repeat to yourself "you get what you pay for if you're very, very lucky."

Conversely, quoting a lower price and not doing the job is a well-known way to rip people off. In either case, the defense is to make sure you're being told a very clear idea or at least somewhat or an idea of what's being done. Most things in life are, in the end, not that complex and can be summarized in a paragraph. The actual process and doing it can be more complicated, but the basic idea shouldn't be that hard to explain to a person of reasonable intelligence and sound memory in an abbreviated form.

Social proof. This, like many ideas in modern

marketing, is derived from pickup and popularized by a guy who went by the pseudonym Mystery. He observed that women respond to a man being the center of attention of a social group (in particular other women) but that even men would boost a person's desirability.

This is apparently a universal human response and an entire industry of semi-fake associations and credentials has emerged. So, be very careful of giving credit to companies when they list other clients or credentials.

The need to act now. This is another trick. If you're being pressured to give a credit card number over the phone I'd recommend against doing business unless they'll send you a written contract.

I've conditioned myself to ask for one and if they say I need to sign up now or their procedure is to record a conversation and get a credit card number I just say "I'm sorry, I guess we can't do business."

## Tracking

The advent of Voice over Internet and fall in call switching cost has led to a further revolution in small business marketing in that tracking has become much easier. You can use a Google Voice number in your Pay Per Click ads. You can also set up an identical site on a different TLD for tracking calls after they arrive at your site (*e.g.* a .net if your main site is a .com). Ringcentral and Callfire offer the ability to get very affordable extra numbers that will allow you to track the incoming calls of any traditional marketing avenue that has a phone number. Callfire can even offer the ability to record calls so you can listen in on calls your receptionist answers to make sure they're bright and cheery.

The biggest problems can come in tracking portal advertising, as effective portals tend to get pulled as Google Places Citations and using an inconsistent tracking number can hinder the process.

## Putting It All Together

At the end of the day the factors that are going to make marketing a local business successful are local and specific. The techiness of an area greatly influences the need to interact in social media. The character of a business itself is also very important.

The two most important factors can be summarized as fun and frequency. Businesses high in these factors will find more benefit in emphasizing social media and find it easier to get reviews. These businesses also typically have a unit charge so customers can need less convincing to try the product, and also might just wander in.

I'd advise all local businesses to start with a website and some basic link building. A good informative website should increase the effectiveness of all other forms of advertising. It's also very cheap.

Then, systematically evaluate all other opportunities in terms of traffic, audience, and cost including both monetary and indirect costs like setup and continued time commitment. Then, try the alternate avenues as time and budget allows.

# Conclusion

Marketing your small business doesn't need to be perplexing. While you need to be aware of interactions, at the end of the day it comes down to cost per sale for any given technique.

I hope you've found this book of use and could leave a decent review. You can email me at david@critwit.com. I will be constructing video tutorials on technical setup of the various tools and techniques in this book on my site http://www.critwit.com. I will also be compiling a resource and site list to accomplish things set out in this book. If you find you need any tutorial in particular, please send me an email and I'll consider putting it on the priority list for video construction.

Thanks for reading.

Very Truly Yours,

David M. Sandy, Esq.

# Short Index

www.ingramcontent.com/pod-product-compliance
Lightning Source LLC
Chambersburg PA
CBHW051318170526
45166CB00002B/594